ktx cd 1
4/97

CW00368820

Penguin Critical Studies

Henry IV Part Two

Neil Taylor, MA (Cantab.), MA (Birmingham), is at present Dean of Arts and Humanities at the Roehampton Institute. Most of his publications have been on Shakespeare and other Elizabethan dramatists.

Penguin Critical Studies
Joint Advisory Editors:
Stephen Coote and Bryan Loughrey

William Shakespeare

Henry IV Part Two

Neil Taylor

Penguin Books

PENGUIN BOOKS

Published by the Penguin Group
27 Wrights Lane, London W8 5TZ, England
Viking Penguin Inc., 40 West 23rd Street, New York, New York 10010, USA
Penguin Books Australia Ltd, Ringwood, Victoria, Australia
Penguin Books Canada Ltd, 10 Alcorn Avenue, Toronto, Ontario, Canada M4V 3B2
Penguin Books (NZ) Ltd, 182–190 Wairau Road, Auckland 10, New Zealand

Penguin Books Ltd, Registered Offices: Harmondsworth, Middlesex, England

First published 1992
10 9 8 7 6 5 4 3 2 1

Copyright © Neil Taylor, 1992
All rights reserved

Filmset in 9/11 pt Monophoto Times

Printed in Great Britain by Clays Ltd, St Ives plc

Except in the United States of America, this book is sold subject to
the condition that it shall not, by way of trade or otherwise, be lent,
re-sold, hired out, or otherwise circulated without the publisher's
prior consent in any form of binding or cover other than that in
which it is published and without a similar condition including this
condition being imposed on the subsequent purchaser

Contents

Introduction   1

1. The Peculiar Structure of the Play   2

2. The Play's Relation to History   5

3. Plot A – the King Plot   12

4. Summary of the Shape and Significance of Plot A   38

5. Plot B – the Falstaff Plot   40

6. Summary of the Shape and Significance of Plot B   71

7. What, No Hal Plot?   72

   Appendix: An Outline of the Multiple Plot   84

   Further Reading   89

Introduction

In the first ten years of his career, Shakespeare wrote eight linked plays about the history of the English monarchy in the fifteenth century. He began with a tetralogy, covering the period 1422–85 (the three parts of *Henry VI* and *Richard III*) and then went back to cover the earlier period, 1398–1420 (*Richard II*, *Henry IV Part One*, *Henry IV Part Two* and *Henry V*).

This Critical Study concentrates on just one of these plays, *Henry IV Part Two*, which Shakespeare composed in 1597. Since he assumes a knowledge of events covered in *Richard II* and *Henry IV Part One*, and since there are many places where the play can be shown to fit into and contribute to patterns of ideas permeating the complete cycle of plays, it is important to read the other seven history plays, and also to read about them. To this end, C. W. R. D. Moseley has written another Penguin Critical Study, *Shakespeare's History Plays* (1988), which forms a companion volume to this book. My intention is not to duplicate his argument but, rather, to follow the complementary principle laid down by the editor of this play in the New Penguin Shakespeare series (1977), P. H. Davison. It is Davison's belief that *Henry IV Part Two* can be studied in isolation, as well as in the context of the other history plays, for it is, as he says, 'a play in its own right, a play of its own kind' (p. 7).

What is distinctive about the play can be analysed in terms of a number of factors. Davison discusses its unique tone (p. 37) and the moral statement it articulates out of its narrative place in relation to the themes of the tetralogy (humanity *v.* authority, pp. 39–40). My approach will necessarily accommodate such a discussion, but I would prefer to take as the foundation of my reading an analysis of the peculiar structure of the play.

1. The Peculiar Structure of the Play

George Eliot wrote in the epigraph to the opening of her novel *Daniel Deronda* that

Man can do nothing without the make-believe of a beginning. Even Science, the strict measurer, is obliged to start with a make-believe unit, and must fix on a point in the stars' unceasing journey when his sidereal clock shall pretend that time is at Nought.

When a historian decides to write a history book s/he is clearly obliged to begin the book at a point within the historical 'story'. Similarly Shakespeare, when he wrote his history plays, had the same decisions to make in relation to his plots and the historical material upon which they were based. He had to decide in which year to place the opening scene of *Henry IV Part Two*. But then it is also the case that when a writer of fictions creates a plot, s/he must appear to be imposing an arbitrary beginning on a pre-existing story which covers more time than the fiction relates. We are told that 'Once upon a time there was a handsome prince . . .' and we therefore imagine that the prince has been living for some time before *this* story begins.

In his book *The Sense of an Ending* (1967), the critic Frank Kermode wrote about how we also need the make-believe of an ending. He argued that the two make-believes are a response to a basic human need to rationalize the experience of living: 'Men . . . to make sense of their span . . . need fictive concords with origins and ends, such as give meaning to lives and to poems' (p. 7). Take the story of Oedipus. It can be told in any number of different ways, according to the points at which the storyteller chooses to begin and end the plot. The Italian poet and film director Pier Paolo Pasolini began his 1967 film *Oedipus Rex* with the birth of Oedipus in Thebes and then showed him later running away from his parents. The playwright Jean Cocteau began his play *The Infernal Machine* (1934) with Oedipus' return to Thebes as an adult, and then showed him answering the sphinx's riddle, being crowned as king and marrying Jocasta. Back in the 420s BC the ancient Greek playwright Sophocles began his play *Oedipus the King* almost at the end of the story, when Oedipus begins to discover the truth about himself and recovers the whole story by piecing together information supplied by a range of participants in and witnesses to it.

2

Sophocles ends the play when Oedipus blinds himself, but the fact that this is not the end of the story is made explicit by the existence of his other play, *Oedipus at Colonus*, which continues the story, showing Oedipus in exile. The ending of a play or a novel or a film is the final determinant of its impact and meaning. Samuel Beckett's *Waiting for Godot* is notorious for the impression it generates that the story has no ending (and no beginning, either). Charles Dickens experimented with different endings to *Great Expectations*, since he was clearly unsatisfied with the effect he was producing by the closing lines. The film of John Fowles's *The French Lieutenant's Woman* follows the spirit of the original novel by offering two alternative endings and suggesting that the audience chooses which it prefers.

The decisions on where to begin and where to end are the author's. But the author inevitably takes notice, consciously or unconsciously, of factors beyond the work of art s/he is composing. In the case of this play, it is designed to fit into a sequence of historical plays, so Shakespeare is also deciding where to end *Henry IV Part One* and where to begin *Henry V*. But he will be taking account of literary conventions too.

One of these is the division of dramatic texts into scenes. Shakespeare breaks up his plot material into twenty-one sections (with the breaks occurring at those points when all the characters have left the stage). The printers of the 1623 Folio edition of his plays labelled these sections, giving the first the description 'Induction', the last 'Epilogue' and the rest act and scene numbers. The five-act division may or may not be helpful, but the division into scenes is, for it alerts us to the fact that Shakespeare has organized the story material into a multiple plot.

The structure of *Henry IV Part Two* has much in common with other plays of its period, and it closely resembles Shakespeare's other histories in many respects. In one very striking respect it imitates the method of its immediate predecessor in the cyc Henry IV Part One. That respect is its adoption of the multiple plot. Many Elizabethan plays have a multiple plot, and Shakespeare used it on a number of occasions. But the double plot of *Henry IV Part Two* is ultimately unlike that of *Henry IV Part One*, and it is in that distinction that much of the distinctiveness of the play resides.

There are as many stories in a work of fiction as we care to find. There is the story of *Henry IV Part Two*, i.e. everything that happens in it, and then there is the story of each character within it. But 'plot' is more than 'story': it is the particular form the storyteller follows. It is the story shaped by the dramatist.

Shakespeare has decided to shape the story of *Henry IV Part Two* so that we are obliged to think of it as a combination of two plots. The pattern is set in I.i and I.ii. The first scene is in blank verse, the second in prose. The first is peopled by one set of characters, the second by another. The first takes place in Northumberland, the second in London. The first is deadly serious, the second comic.

They seem to be two distinctive worlds. And if we look further into the play, we can see that this oppositional relationship is persevered with. Scenes I.i and iii, II.iii, III.i, IV.i, ii, iv and v, and V.ii are in verse, and deal with incidents in the political life of the nation. They are set either in the palace or else on the battlefield. They are serious in mood and follow the fortunes of the King, his struggle against rebel forces in the land, his worries about the succession, his death and the accession of a new king. Scenes I.ii, II.i, ii and iv, III.ii, IV.iii and V.i, iii and iv are almost entirely in prose and all concern Falstaff and his circle of friends. They are comic in tone and set in a variety of locations – the street, the tavern, Shallow's home, the battlefield.

Clearly there is a distinction being drawn between the spheres of the ruler and the ruled. There is also a distinction between history and fiction, for Shakespeare has taken the incidents of the first set of scenes largely from history books, whereas he has invented the incidents in the second set for himself.

It will be the procedure of this book to discuss the play in two stages. First, I shall divide the play into its constituent plots and provide a commentary on each. The 'historical' scenes focusing on the King I shall call plot A; the 'fictional' scenes focusing on Falstaff I shall call plot B. Secondly, I shall turn to the play as a whole and analyse its procedures as an integrated multiple plot. However, before embarking on the first stage, it is necessary to consider the supposed distinction between history and fiction invoked in the preceding paragraph.

2. The Play's Relation to History

Shakespeare *writes plays*. But we also refer to him as a *playwright*. The verb 'write' somehow suggests the creation of new material, for when we write on a page we make something appear that was not there before. But the noun 'wright' means a maker, and in particular a carpenter or joiner. A man who makes a ship or wheel (a shipwright or a wheelwright) joins and shapes wood, pre-existing material.

The coincidence of two words with such different associations is actually instructive of how we conceive of a dramatist like Shakespeare. For in one sense we feel that a dramatist is selecting, arranging, joining together and shaping material – making a plot out of story material. And this is how my discussion of plot has thus far proceeded. But in another sense it is nonsense to think of Shakespeare's material having a pre-existence, for has he not invented every word that is in *Henry IV Part Two* (after all, people in real life do not speak in blank verse) and isn't *Henry IV Part Two* entirely made up of words?

The same problem arises with words themselves. It is automatic for most of us to assume that our ideas have an existence before we put them into words. Yet we also know (and modern linguistics asserts it insistently) that ideas are inseparable from the words in which they are expressed and that, as we sometimes discover, we do not know what we are going to say until we have said it!

What complicates this problem in the case of a play like *Henry IV Part Two* is the fact that its story purports to give an account of the last years of the reign of a real, historical figure, King Henry IV. Quite clearly there is pre-existing material here, which Shakespeare can be said to be shaping. But we have to be careful. The material that predates the play is of different kinds. The reign of Henry IV took place years before Shakespeare wrote of it. Henry IV is long dead. His reign is only an idea. It has no substance any longer and therefore, unless we give it one, no shape.

Shakespeare's access to it could only have been through other people's accounts of it. Their shape is not the reign's shape. History is story, an account of past events with a pattern which is not *in* the events but *attributed* to them. Every historian's account of that reign is necessarily going to be different and provide a different pattern.

Nevertheless we inevitably *feel* that the past has an existence to which an historian attempts to be true. A modern historian's pursuit of truth incorporates a methodology, the recovery of the earliest authentic documentation of the past and then the rational interpretation of the incidents recovered from that documentation. Shakespeare was not a historian, and in so far as he was writing a kind of history his methodology would not prove acceptable to a modern historian. For Shakespeare seems to have used, not early documents, but recent history books, most notably a book published in 1587 (the second edition of Raphael Holinshed's *Chronicles of England, Scotland, and Ireland*), i.e. only ten years before he wrote his play.

So the material Shakespeare was shaping was clearly not the reign of Henry IV. It was accounts of that reign. And his purpose in writing about the reign was not one of pure, historical scholarship. He was writing a play, not a history book. His motives in writing the play may have included the attempt to be true to the past, but they certainly included other motives too.

Furthermore, not only in the a-historical scenes (i.e. the Falstaff scenes of plot B) but in some other areas of plot A too, Shakespeare's material, in so far as it had a pre-existence and could therefore be regarded as a 'source', went beyond history books and included such things as the Bible and plays performed or read earlier in Elizabeth's reign.

Let us, therefore, begin by considering what a modern historian's account of Henry IV's reign would look like.

The Reign of Henry IV

Henry Bolingbroke's father was John of Gaunt, Duke of Lancaster, and his grandfather was King Edward III. Edward III's eldest son, the Black Prince, died in 1376 so that, when Edward himself died the following year, it was the Black Prince's son who succeeded to the throne and became King Richard II. Henry was thus the first cousin of the king. But in 1398 Richard sent him into exile and on the almost immediate death of John of Gaunt, confiscated the Lancastrian estates and thereby denied Henry his inheritance. Henry invaded England in 1399, ostensibly to claim his title as Duke of Lancaster, but the effect was to force Richard's abdication. Henry thus became King Henry IV.

Henry's right to the throne was disputed. While the Black Prince was the eldest son, John of Gaunt was the *third* son. The second son, Lionel, had died in 1368, leaving only a daughter. She and her husband, Edmund Mortimer, Earl of March, died in 1381 but the childless Richard II named their son, Roger, as his heir. Roger was murdered in Ireland in 1398 but he left an heir, the six-year old Edmund Mortimer. Clearly there was a strong case for regarding him as the rightful king of England when Richard abdicated in 1399.

Henry nevertheless managed to secure the throne. But until 1409 he had his work cut out holding on to it. Henry's problems were concerned with two issues: (a) the defence of the realm and the maintenance of his own authority within it and (b) the raising of money to pay for (a). The external enemies were France and Scotland, but Henry had also to face internal military opposition from Wales and the north of England.

These rebellions arose from three kinds of grievance: (a) Welsh dislike of English rule, leading to military risings every summer from 1400 to 1408; (b) quarrels (over money and the ransom of prisoners) between Henry and one of his chief sources of political support, the Percy family; (c) the cause of young Edmund Mortimer.

In 1403 there was an attempt to have Edmund crowned as king. It was made by the Percies, who had risen to prominence during Richard's reign and were now the most powerful family in the north of England. Henry Percy had been created Earl of Northumberland in 1377. His brother was created Earl of Worcester in 1397. But Northumberland and his son Henry 'Hotspur' Percy shifted allegiance to Henry of Bolingbroke the moment he invaded England in 1399. Worcester deserted Richard in Ireland, and Northumberland captured Richard for Henry while the king was coming back through Wales. The Percies were rewarded by the new king for their support, but within four years had turned against him.

One reason for their revolt was Henry's inability to furnish them with sufficient funds to defend the border lands where they were based. When in 1402 they repelled a Scottish army at Homildon Hill in Yorkshire and captured the Scottish leader, the Earl of Douglas, Hotspur refused to hand over his prisoner to the king, arguing that Henry owed them money. Henry had already alienated Hotspur by refusing to ransom Hotspur's brother-in-law, who had fallen into rebel hands in Wales. (This brother-in-law was Sir Edmund Mortimer, the uncle of the little boy whose claims to the throne the Percies then began to advance, calculating that their own political influence would be thereby increased.)

The chief source of military opposition to Henry in Wales was from Owen Glendower. Henry's son Henry (Hal) was Prince of Wales and as such had his hands full trying to cope with Glendower. In 1402 Glendower's prisoner, Sir Edmund Mortimer, joined forces with him, having married his daughter. In 1403, while the king was marching north to give support to Northumberland against the Scots, he heard the news that Hotspur had raised an army in Cheshire and was planning to attack Hal's troops at Shrewsbury. Hotspur's prisoner, Douglas, was now fighting with him, and Hotspur had support, either actual or theoretical, from his uncle Worcester, his father Northumberland, a Cheshire landowner, Sir Richard Vernon, Glendower and Sir Edmund Mortimer. The battle at Shrewsbury lasted the whole of 21 July. Hal was wounded but Hotspur was killed, Worcester and Vernon were captured and executed, and Douglas was held prisoner for five years.

Most of what has just been recounted covers the period portrayed in *Henry IV Part One*. *Part Two* opens at the moment when the first reports of the battle of Shrewsbury have begun to emanate from the battlefield. Shakespeare turns immediately to the next phase of political and military unrest, the rebellion in the north.

For some time the Archbishop of York (Richard Scrope or Scroop) had been giving support to those who opposed the king (his brother was married into the Percy family). Scroop's position is a confusing one. Richard II had appointed him archbishop, and Henry had executed his cousin. Yet he had appeared to be behind Henry's cause, assisting in his enthronement and lending him money. In the spring of 1405, however, he drew up a document protesting, among other things, at the king's punitive taxation of the commons and assault upon the dignity of the clergy. In May, he became leader of another military rebellion in the north, assisted by Thomas, Lord Bardolph, and the young Earl of Norfolk, Thomas Mowbray. His army was assembled near Gaultree Forest in Yorkshire when the Earl of Westmorland (Ralph Neville, one of the king's oldest supporters) appeared. He had just defeated an army of Northumberland's men who were marching to join Scroop. After three days Westmorland made an offer of peace, promising to discuss and deal with the issues raised by Scroop's document. The rebel leaders were tricked into dismissing their army and then arrested. As a cleric Scroop should have been tried by an ecclesiastical court but Henry, arriving a few days later, ignored the law, appointed a judicial commission, and saw to it that Scroop was beheaded.

In the meantime, Mortimer and Glendower had signed an agreement with Northumberland. It was their intention to oust Henry and then divide up the country between the three of them. (Glendower's success was such that by 1405 he was seeking national independence for Wales and had advanced into England as far as Worcester before he was beaten back by Henry and his army. This was the year of Glendower's

8

major threat to the king and he thereafter lost ground and significance.) But after Scroop's execution Northumberland escaped into Scotland for the summer before attempting to gather support for a further assault on the king. This was launched in February 1408, when Northumberland marched down to Bramham Moor, but there he was fatally wounded in an encounter with the sheriff of Yorkshire. Soon after, the Welsh revolt petered out and Henry could finally rule in peace.

The years 1408 to 1413 were a period in which Henry was in command of his country but plagued by illness. Hal had been active in the defence of his father's rule since 1399 when, at the age of twelve, he had been made nominal head of the governing council of Wales. In his early teens he had been fighting Welsh rebels. Now he was responsible for Calais and the major ports on the English side of the Channel, and managed to advance English interests in France through a blend of belligerence and diplomacy. At some points in the last six years of the king's life Hal's was the most powerful voice on the king's council. In 1411, however, his uncle Henry Beaufort, Bishop of Winchester, suggested that the king abdicate in favour of Hal and the king responded by removing Hal from his council. It took a year or more for father and son to become reconciled. During the last three months of the king's life Hal gradually assumed authority, and his father died in March 1413.

Shakespeare's Sources

Shakespeare knew of Henry IV's reign from a variety of sources, some of which we have access to but some of which (including what he heard rather than read) we will no doubt never be able to trace. The book he seems to have used extensively throughout the whole of his English history cycle was Raphael Holinshed's *The Chronicles of England, Scotland, and Ireland* (second edition, 1587). This was partly dependent upon an earlier work, Edward Hale's *The Union of the Two Noble and Illustre Families of Lancaster and York* (1548), but Shakespeare may well have consulted both books. He also seems to have read Samuel Daniel's lengthy poem entitled *The First Four Books of the Civil Wars between the Two Houses of Lancaster and York* (1595).

As with all works of history, each of these tells a 'story'. Elizabethan history was rooted in Polydore Vergil's *Anglica Historia* (1534) – a history of England commissioned by Elizabeth I's grandfather, Henry VII. Vergil reads the history of the fifteenth century as a troubled period which only the accession of Henry VII himself had successfully ended. This obviously reflects the conditions under which Vergil was writing, but he could hardly help being influenced by previous historians and, as H. A. Kelly has explained (in *Divine Providence in the England of Shakespeare's Histories*, 1970), the period 1399–1485 provided the humanist historians of the early Renaissance with three 'myths' – a Lancastrian myth (Bolingbroke was an agent of divine justice when he overthrew the corrupt Richard II and God rewarded him and his pious son with triumphs at home and abroad), a Yorkist myth (Bolingbroke was a criminal for overthrowing Richard II and God punished him for it when his grandson, Henry VI, yielded up the throne to the Yorkists), and a Tudor myth (although God supported the Lancastrians, the Yorkists were rewarded and the country blessed when Henry VII married Elizabeth of York in 1486).

Graham Holderness cites Kelly's book in his *Shakespeare's History* (1985) and maintains (p. 22) that such a range of myths meant that

An intelligent humanist account like Vergil's could choose from a wide range of interpretations and construct a narrative which, despite its attempt to subsume all ... details into an overriding providential pattern, contains much awareness and evidence of the ideological conflicts which naturally characterized the period under discussion. This is so even in the chronicle of Halle, which is conventionally regarded as the major source of the providential theory of the history of England from 1399 to 1485, and of the Tudor myth. Halle in fact was himself extremely sceptical about providential explanations of history. And it is particularly the case in Holinshed, whose encyclopaedic method of compilation gives a very full representation to diverse and contradictory accounts.

So, in constructing the plot of *Henry IV Part Two*, Shakespeare was reworking and developing previous narrative material. As Holderness goes on to argue (pp. 22–3)

every 'understanding' of history is to some degree ideological, and the providential theory embodied in the Tudor myth was particularly adept at incorporating contradictions – no event, however unpredictable or apparently the result of an arbitrary and capricious chance, can resist explanation in terms of an overriding divine will, mediated through the complex machinery of 'fortune' and the 'secondary causes' of human action.

An important example of the exploitation of this kind of thinking is a collection of moral tales in verse which Shakespeare probably consulted, William Baldwin's *A Mirror for Magistrates* (1559). Baldwin tells the stories of political leaders ('magistrates') whose falls from power illustrate either their own depravity or else the operations of Fortune in an unpredictable world. Both Richard II and the Earl of Northumberland (whom Shakespeare portrays in *Richard II, Henry IV Part One* and *Henry IV Part Two*) have their stories told. The title of the book explains its didactic purpose. It is a mirror in which rulers can peer in order to see the dangers inherent in their situation – 'with howe grevous plages vices are punished: and howe frayle and unstable worldly prosperitie is founde'. The *Mirror* was a popular work (it was reissued in 1563, 1578 and 1587, each time expanded by the addition of new stories) and its direct influence can be detected in some of Shakespeare's plays. Its importance here lies in the fact that it exemplifies Elizabethan interest, not only in the didactic uses of history, but also in the role and responsibilities of the ruler, the magistrate, the governor. And in this respect it is worth noting that *Henry IV Part Two* derives some of the story of Hal's misspent youth from Sir Thomas Elyot's *The Book Named the Governor* (1531), which sets out to describe the moral and practical qualities expected of the ideal ruler.

We have already moved some way from academic chronicle history, and we need to move still further. Some part of Shakespeare's knowledge of, and attitudes to, Henry IV's reign probably derives from at least one popular play staged in one of the new public playhouses. In about 1594 the anonymous *Famous Victories of Henry the Fifth* dramatized the incident in which the young Hal strikes the Lord Chief Justice – an incident Shakespeare assumes knowledge of, even though he does not present it directly. Another anonymous work, *Tarlton's Jests* (1608), refers to 'a play of *Henry the Fifth*, wherein the judge was to take a box on the ear' and mentions that it was performed 'At the Bull in Bishopsgate'. Tarlton, the clown, died in 1588, and he is supposed by this anecdote to have been present at the performance, so it is quite possible that Shakespeare's conception of Hal was affected by yet another theatrical source.

3. Plot A – the King Plot

Shakespeare's 'Alterations' of History in Plot A

Sometimes Shakespeare seems to have altered history by mistake. (The 'Kent' whom he introduces in the Quarto headnote to IV.iv died five years before this incident. But he says nothing anyway.) On the whole, though, the departures from his sources seem deliberate and intelligible. Henry IV reigned from 1399 to 1413, i.e. for fourteen years. For eight of these years he was struggling to keep his country in order, but for the last five years of his rule he was fairly firmly in control. Shakespeare shapes this material in two major ways. Firstly, he creates the impression that once the battle of Shrewsbury had been won (1403) Henry became almost exclusively concerned with his spiritual and physical ill health, rather than the political and military troubles which in fact continued for another five years. Secondly, he forgets about the next, and final, five years of Henry's reign, which were a period of relative stability and peace.

The decision to concentrate on the first phase of the reign at the expense of the second provided Shakespeare with a unified reading of Henry's reign: it became, in a phrase used by the Lord Chief Justice at I.ii.152, 'th'unquiet time'. This act of shaping can already be detected in Holinshed, and Hall made the title of the relevant section of his history 'The Unquiet Time of King Henry the Fourth'; this was then taken up in Holinshed's title, 'King Henry's Unquiet Reign'.

As Peter Saccio points out (in *Shakespeare's English Kings: History, Chronicle and Drama*, 1977), Shakespeare moves the compact between Percy, Mortimer and Glendower (to divide the country in three) into *Henry IV Part One* just before Shrewsbury, thereby making *Henry IV Part Two* 'a little thin in political substance' (p. 52). But Shakespeare makes sure that Percy is seen both as a threat and as a villain. In I.i Northumberland is shown to be 'crafty-sick' (Rumour's phrase, Induction, 37). He is persuaded by his wife to flee before Scroop encounters Prince John's army (II.iii). The historical facts are otherwise: Percy was probably genuinely ill, his wife was dead and he escaped a full month after Scroop's execution. Shakespeare's Percy is not only a coward but an embodiment of destructive evil. In I.i.154 Northumberland vows that he will bring chaos to the land, let loose 'the wild flood', and 'Let order die'.

But Shakespeare, as I say, describes an unquietness which is not only political but psychological as well. By telescoping time Shakespeare makes Henry seem always older and sicker than in fact he was during most of the years covered by the play. Indeed, he had introduced Henry's wish to go on a penitential crusade at the very beginning of his reign (*Richard II*, V.vi.49–50: 'I'll make a voyage to the Holy Land,/ To wash this blood off from my guilty hand') rather than at the end. Once again, however, the origin of this conception of personal unquietness may come from Shakespeare's sources. The emphasis he places on the King's distressed and guilty state of mind could well have been influenced by the account of Henry's reign contained in Daniel. And as well as sharing the emphasis, they even use similar imagery at one point: Daniel talks of pain and grief 'Wearing the wall so thin that now the mind Might well looke thorow, and his frailty find' (iii.116), while Clarence says 'Th'incessant care and labour of his mind/Hath wrought the mure that should confine it in/So thin that life looks through and will break out' (*Henry IV Part Two*, IV.iv.118–20).

A further piece of shaping lies in Shakespeare's handling of Prince John and Prince Hal. He eliminates the King and the judicial commission from the Gaultree episode, emphasizing and elaborating on the trick that it played on the rebels and reassigning responsibility for it to Prince John rather than to Westmorland. This darkens the character of John (whom Shakespeare erroneously calls the Duke of Lancaster) and makes him a foil to Hal.

Meanwhile, Shakespeare makes of Hal a more noble and heroic and virtuous character than historical documents proclaim him. It is not an established fact that Hal killed Hotspur at the battle of Shrewsbury, though Holinshed seems to say that he did (his phrasing is slightly ambiguous). Shakespeare makes it a key event in *Henry IV Part One* and harks back to it in *Henry IV Part Two* (e.g. Morton at I.i.105–11).

Perhaps more significantly, Shakespeare omits to mention that in 1412, during the final, peaceful phase of Henry IV's reign, Hal was involved in a bid to force Henry to abdicate in his favour. Shakespeare does not include the Bishop of Winchester or the Earl of Arundel in the cast list of this play. It was their support which influenced the historical Hal to pressurize his father into abdicating. The third of the supporters, Richard Beauchamp, Earl of Warwick, is included but not in the role of such a counsellor, and even here Shakespeare goes wrong for, on one occasion, he refers to him as 'Nevil' (III.i.62), which was the surname of the Earl of Westmorland. Holinshed tells us how Hal tried to reassure his father that there was no plot against him, by offering the king a dagger and inviting him to kill him (possibly Shakespeare was influenced by this when he gave the King IV.v.107–10).

Finally, Shakespeare makes one of the most significant events of *Henry IV Part Two* Hal's decisions (*a*) to acknowledge the Lord Chief Justice's right and duty to have imprisoned him and (*b*) to reconfirm the Lord Chief Justice in his post. The first decision is obviously unsupported by history in so far as we have established that there is no evidence of Hal's ever having been imprisoned. The second decision is quite bogus: Henry V did *not* reappoint his father's Lord Chief Justice.

Plot A as Shakespeare Handles It

INDUCTION

> Rebellion in this land shall lose his sway,
> Meeting the check of such another day,
> And since this business so fair is done,
> Let us not leave till all our own be won.
>
> (*Henry IV Part One*, V.v.41–4)

So ends *Henry IV Part One*. The King's speech, coming as it does at the close of the play and organized around such insistent rhyming couplets, makes us feel that rebellion is crushed, and that the battle of Shrewsbury has been the climax and the resolution of the play's dramatic energies. But, if we listen to the speech carefully we realize that Shrewsbury has not yet brought all the King's subjects to order. Prince John and the Earl of Westmorland must march north to deal with Northumberland and Archbishop Scroop, the King and Hal must march west to deal with Glendower and the Earl of March in Wales. We are left with conflicting information – dramatic information which suggests closure, intellectual information which resists closure.

The Induction to *Henry IV Part Two* takes up the same material, the historical material of plot A, the King plot. But it deals with it through a character, Rumour, who operates simultaneously in a number of different discourses, some of which extend into the other plot, B, as well.

One of these discourses is clearly that of historical fact, for he quickly alludes to the battle of Shrewsbury in 1403.

> *My office is*
> *To noise abroad that Harry Monmouth fell*
> *Under the wrath of noble Hotspur's sword,*
> *And that the King before the Douglas' rage*
> *Stooped his anointed head as low as death.*

(28–32)

Thus, he introduces truth (historical reality) and at the same time untruth (he is going to lie). This is the opening speech. Rumour's view is the first information we are given. We are told what to believe, and we are also told to believe nothing. The speech teaches scepticism, it warns against gullibility and too easy trust.

But Rumour also invokes the world of imaginative literature. He has many of the characteristics of the traditional villains in the popular drama of the Elizabethan period. His use of *direct address* to the audience recreates the conventional relationship of the Vice with the audience in the medieval morality plays. His naked scheming and lying are characteristic of a self-confessed Machiavel, like Barabas in Christopher Marlowe's *The Jew of Malta*. Two or three years earlier Shakespeare had begun his own play, *Richard III*, with just such an opening speech from the machiavellian Richard.

The very first information we are given, '*Enter Rumour, painted full of tongues*', links Rumour to Fama (Fame), an allegorical figure used by Virgil and Ovid in Roman literature, and depicted by Renaissance writers in the sixteenth century as wearing a costume decorated with tongues or eyes or ears. Rumour and Fame may be compared to an actor addressing an audience – they deal in falsehoods eagerly believed.

Indeed, it is our own vulnerability to deceit and false trust that is going to be explored. 'Open your ears,' Rumour commands, and we do, 'for which of you will stop/ The vent of hearing when loud Rumour speaks?' (1–2). Rumour is playing with us by offering us himself as something to be played upon. 'I thus/ My well-known body ... anatomize/ Among my household' (20–22) The paradoxes continue. Let me introduce myself as someone you already know! I am going to conduct an anatomy lesson on myself! We know now that we are not dealing with mere history. Rumour is an abstraction, a personification, and we are encouraged to employ a type of thinking which is non-naturalistic and even intellectual. It is going to be moral history and we must be prepared to think allegorically as well as literally and naturalistically.

Rumour also introduces some major themes which the play as a whole explores. For example, we are told that the setting of I.i will be a 'worm-eaten hold of raggèd stone/ Where Hotspur's father, old

15

Northumberland,/ Lies crafty-sick' (35–7), 'Worm-eaten' and 'raggèd' create an impression of decay and of the degenerative effects of time. At the same time, 'crafty' prepares us not only for a rebel but for a deceiver, and the theme of deception is reinforced by the very nature of the Induction itself.

Rumour is arrogant, boastful, blustering and bombastic, noisy, bustling, active, energetic, violent, 'loud'. Rumour deals in melodrama, tales of false pregnancies, substanceless panic about war, hyperbole and then bathos. He leads us straight into I.i. But his sound and fury will also make an interesting contrast to the lassitude and enervation of the other world, the world of plot B, which is introduced in I.ii. In the meantime, though, we remember the final thoughts which Rumour crams into our ears. (And we may recall the witches who open *Macbeth* and prepare the way for the entry of the individuated mortals with whom they have a similarly ambiguous power-relation – we may wonder whether Northumberland and Henry, like Macbeth and Duncan, control their own destinies or are controlled by supernatural forces. We are confused now as to whether the historical figures we are about to observe will be in control of their lives or, being figures of history, are subject to the power of History. And, since Shakespeare has made his opening character Rumour, and suggested that the audience's relation to his character is characteristic of our relationship to rumours (and that Fame is yet another analogue), we wonder too about the power-relations and the operations of trust in relation to 'news', 'fame', 'reputation' and 'art'. 'False' and 'true' ring in our ears in much the same way as 'fair' and 'foul' ring in our ears after the first scene of *Macbeth*.)

Play and war, false and true. The contrasts are harsh, the tone is brash and bullying, the attitudes cynical and demeaning. We are lumped in with that 'blunt monster with uncounted heads,/ The still-discordant wavering multitude' (18–19). The voice is treacherous – 'I speak of peace while covert enmity,/ Under the smile of safety, wounds the world' (9–10). It speaks falteringly of 'young Hotspur' as 'noble Hotspur' (25, 30). But it is not that Rumour is in the pay of the rebel camp. The treachery it performs will strike at the rebel it has already libelled, Hotspur's father, the Earl of Northumberland.

ACT I, SCENE i

The setting is a gate. Rumour presented himself as somebody communicating and mediating information. The Porter at the gate of

Northumberland's citadel has the same intermediary function, representing the inside world to the outside world and vice versa.

The scene proves to be confused but full of energy and activity – entrances, bustle, desperation, desire. But Northumberland is shut away in his orchard, having escaped into supposed illness and a private, domestic, pastoral world. (We might compare it with that of Shallow later in the play and, elsewhere in Shakespeare, Brutus' orchard or Prospero's island.) He has shut out the world of war and the flow of history, that world which he has abandoned out of cowardice or craft, the world in which his son has fought and, as we know but he does not, died. So we are confronted with a man isolated in a world of his imagination.

But his imagination is ripe with ideas about the outside world and he is eager for news. Not only does he leap ahead anticipating good news (13) but, continuing Rumour's image of the development of news and rumour as being like pregnancy and birth, Northumberland talks of every minute as if it should be 'the father of some stratagem' (8). This, though, is a perverse image. Rumour's pregnancy proved a phantom pregnancy ('And no such matter', line 15), Northumberland's leads to abortion ('stratagem' = 'violent and bloody act', according to Davison in the Penguin edition of the play).

He is misled into believing that the King is dying of wounds incurred in the battle, that Prince John and Westmorland and Stafford are in flight, and that Hotspur has killed Hal and taken Falstaff prisoner (in this last fiction, the world of plot B is momentarily introduced). He believes it because his source, 'A gentleman well bred, and of good name' (26), claimed to have acquired the information at Shrewsbury. Bardolph discredits Travers's source, rejecting the man's social standing – he must have been 'Some hilding fellow that had stolen/ The horse he rode on, and, upon my life,/ Spoke at a venture' (57–9). We notice how all the 'news' is rumour, second- or even third-hand, and we notice how truth and public standing are elided.

The truth, therefore, is no simple matter. Northumberland has to interpret the words of his messengers, to 'read' them: 'Yea, this man's brow, like to a title-leaf,/ Foretells the nature of a tragic volume' (60–61). He reads Morton's face like a book. For his part, Morton read Shrewsbury like a play: 'hateful death put on his ugliest mask/ To fright our party' (66–7). Even Northumberland's allusion to the sack of Troy involves a mediating figure: a servant (Shakespeare's invention, for he is not present in *The Iliad* or *The Aeneid*) who draws back Priam's curtain like a character in an Elizabethan play 'discovering' a tableau in the inner stage. At every point the imagery has stressed mediation and interpretation, the reading of signs. Yet everything Northumberland says confirms the power of words. Morton hesitates, Northumberland knows, but the ritual of affirmation has to be completed.

Morton's imagery helps focus attention on the play's concern with the quality of life. Rumour has told how Hal 'Hath beaten down young Hotspur and his troops,/ Quenching the flame of bold rebellion' (Induction, 25–6). Morton pursues the same metaphor. Hal's

> swift wrath beat down
> *The never-daunted Percy to the earth,*
> *From whence with life he never more sprung up.*

(I.i.109–11)

The beating down in the Induction seemed a reaction to an attack, like beating off a dog or stamping down an outbreak of fire in undergrowth. Now it seems more tyrannical and callous, a brutal denial of life and spirit. The Induction's phrase 'bold rebellion' was ambiguous – 'bold' suggesting impertinence as much as courage – but here 'The never-daunted Percy' seems heroic. Of course, Morton *would* be presenting him thus to his father. But the speech is long (105–35) and most of it is given over to the development of these metaphors. *Life* and *spirit* and *fire spring up* and would fly. They are opposed by the *dull, labouring heavy weight* of *enforcement* and repression. We are alerted to the issue of energy and life, how they are at stake and would be denied, but also how much the quality of life matters. We witness intense activity, but we feel that Rumour's bustle was not attractive, and neither, once it is activated by Morton's news, is Northumberland's demonic energy.

When Northumberland first entered he was supposedly sick. On the Elizabethan stage this could be indicated semiotically by the wearing of some article of nightwear during the day. In this case the supposed soldier is wearing his nightcap. Now, like an actor changing costume, he throws it off:

> hence, thou sickly coif!
> *Thou art a guard too wanton for the head*
> *Which princes, fleshed with conquest, aim to hit.*
> *Now bind my brows with iron, and approach*
> *The raggèd'st hour that time and spite dare bring*
> *To frown upon th'enraged Northumberland!*

(147–52)

By means of this gesture Northumberland declares himself to be well rather than ill. But he also adopts the role of the soldier (signified by the helmet rather than the nightcap), the revenger (the father avenging the death of his son – like Hieronimo in Thomas Kyd's *The Spanish Tragedy*, or Titus in Shakespeare's own early play, *Titus Andronicus*), and the man of courage rather than the coward. Finally, in this gesture of throwing off the coif Northumberland reverts to the pattern of order rather than disorder, for he has been dressed for night and now he will adopt the costume of day along with everyone else.

Northumberland's own account of this transformation is not as simple as that he was one thing and now he is the opposite. He deals in paradox. 'In poison,' he says, 'there is physic.' Given the right 'measure' of certain poisons, he remembers, certain illnesses can be cured. There is an order in which disorder can create order. Northumberland revives the image of fire. Again it is part of a paradox. A man sick with fever is hot and feels he is on fire. But, sick of his sickness ('Impatient of his fit'), he breaks away from his nurse just as fire will suddenly break out (140–43) when you think it is quenched. The mind, the spirit which Morton described as fled, revives in Northumberland and revitalizes the body. And we see it happen, for he throws away his crutch and walks.

However, all this is intellectually undermined by our knowledge of Rumour's accusation that Northumberland is only 'crafty-sick'. If we reread the scene in the light of this idea, Northumberland is only deciding to act a new part. Can we really disentangle the two readings? Perhaps grief and rage have mended a spiritual sickness and Northumberland has genuinely reverted to a life of order. But 'Let order die!' (154), he exclaims. He could simply mean, let the current political order, i.e. the rule of Henry IV, be ended. But his sentiments in the lines around these three words are an attack upon the very order of the universe: 'Now let not Nature's hand/ Keep the wild flood confined!' (153–4); in other words, let the rivers break their banks, let the sea invade the land, let there be another Flood! If he wishes to reinvoke the Flood, then he is turning the cosmic clock back too, so he would disorder time: '. . . let one spirit of the first-born Cain/ Reign in all bosoms' (157–8). This is to put the clock back almost to the Garden of Eden. (Northumberland is in his orchard at the beginning of this scene.) But the spirit of Cain is the spirit of the first murderer, the brother-murderer.

Northumberland would identify himself with the first criminal. And, to make his invocation of disorder complete, he would upset the physical

19

order of the universe ('Let heaven kiss earth!', line 153) and take away God's first act, the creation of light. 'Let there be light' were God's words, but Northumberland's are 'Let order die . . . darkness be' (160).

Revealingly, Northumberland also employs the imagery of theatre:

> And let this world no longer be a stage
> To feed contention in a lingering act;
> But let . . .
>   the rude scene . . . end,
> And darkness be the burier of the dead!

(155–60)

At the same time as he would reverse the order of time and take us back to the primeval chaos, the time before time, Northumberland would take us apocalyptically *forward* to the end of time. In theatrical terms he would accelerate time, hurrying us on through the lingering act to the last scene of a tragedy, when the stage is littered with bodies, the audience has gone home and darkness falls on the public stage.

This is glorious histrionic stuff, with Northumberland blasphemously parodying and perverting God's word and deconstructing every dimension of order – spatial, temporal and moral. But the self-referential theatricality of it makes it seem, to Bardolph at least, too much like the histrionics of a bad actor: 'This strainèd passion doth you wrong, my lord' (161).

Northumberland's imagination had re-introduced the image of feeding (156). In Bardolph's next speech there is mention of choking (184), and Morton then goes on to talk of queasiness (196) and gasping (208) (having introduced an allusion to the stomach much earlier, at line 129). The contexts suggest no consistency of thought with respect to these images, but we recall Northumberland's image of 'Stopping my greedy ear' (78) and we think back to Travers's source, who rode off almost instantly and 'seemed in running to devour the way' (47). If we recall Rumour 'stuffing the ears of men' (Induction, 8) and his image of the 'big year [*sic*], swollen' (Induction 13), an indistinct composite image of desire, gluttony and nausea emerges.

ACT I, SCENE iii

The focus of the rebellion has shifted from Northumberland to Scroop, the Archbishop of York, whom we meet for the first time. For all

Northumberland's blustering rhetoric he has proved to be neither the Machiavel nor the Vice. He seems, rather, to be turning out the Braggart – another stock character from the drama, this time deriving from classical comedy (the plays, that is, of the Roman dramatists Terence and Plautus), already utilized by Shakespeare in the person of Don Armado in *Love's Labour's Lost*.

The scene raises and briefly develops the play's discussion of the imagination. There is agreement among the rebels present over the force and justice of their 'cause' (though we are denied the chance to test these out), but doubts over the adequacy of their 'means' (i.e. the strength of their armies). They have 25,000 troops without North-umberland's army. This is probably not enough. If he joins them, Bardolph believes they are strong enough, but until he does Bardolph prefers to hold back. Scroop concurs, arguing that 'Conjecture, expecta-tion, and surmise' (23) are not to be trusted. Hotspur put his faith in hope and look what happened to him. What is hope? It is mere *imagin-ation* (31). It is a matter of 'Eating the air' (28), it is self-flattery (29), it is shutting your eyes to the truth – 'winking' (33). Imagination is 'Proper to madmen' (in *A Midsummer Night's Dream* Shakespeare lumped together as victims of the imagination 'the lunatic, the lover, and the poet'). Bardolph argues down Hastings, who feels they *must* use their imaginations in order to plan and hypothesize – how else is military strategy to be conceived?

Towards the end of I.i, Bardolph has compared rebellion to the heroic voyage of a merchant venturer. Now, shifting from one com-mercial field to another, he compares a revolutionary to a builder, demolishing one house in order to build another, drawing up plans and imagining the new house *in situ*. If it looks to be too costly he goes back to the drawing-board and imagines a less ambitious structure. The rebels too must do their sums, and their unit of currency is the soldier. However, Hastings wins the debate, for he persuades the others that 25,000 men is enough to take on the King. The King's troops have to fight on three fronts: one division fights the French, one (under the King and Hal, so they believe) fights the Welsh, and only the third (under Prince John and Westmorland) is left to fight them. The King can hire no more soldiers for he is bankrupt.

There is little charity in Scroop's religion. He is full of contempt for the common people, who are insatiable in their greed and fickle in their political loyalties. Gluttony is a moral sickness which leads to literal sickness – they vomit up one leader and swallow the next; surfeited with their 'over-greedy love' (88), like dogs they re-devour their own vomit. But as well as extending the imagery of unhealthy eating Scroop revives the image of politics as theatre. The people once eagerly applauded Bolingbroke as a new star actor striding on to the political stage. Now they are bored with him and hungry for novelty. The rebels must cash in.

ACT II, SCENE iii

Northumberland, the rebel and the soldier, the supposed leader of men, is discovered in the middle of a domestic row. And what is he quarrelling about? Honour. His wife and daughter-in-law wish him to stay at home, he argues that his honour obliges him to go to war.

The irony of his debating the male, chivalric concept with two women is intensified by the fact that Northumberland's honour is already suspect. In our eyes, it is tarnished by Rumour's description of him as 'crafty-sick' (Induction, 37). Significantly employing the imagery of bourgeois commerce, he protests 'my honour is at pawn,/ And but my going, nothing can redeem it' (7–8). But Lady Percy argues that, when he failed to turn up at the battle of Shrewsbury and his son was killed, two honours were lost – the son's noble, heroic life, and the father's good name and reputation.

Hotspur's reputation (his *fama*) was spread throughout the kingdom. He was the type, the form, the 'book' (31) of fashion. The youth of England acted him, like a character in a play, and so, 'Did all the chivalry of England move/ To do brave acts' (20–21). That was the past, the days when heroic acts of chivalry were practised. But those chivalric days are gone. Northumberland is on the spot in the present. He argues pragmatically, but with failing spirit (46), that he must take the opportunity (see I.iii) or else lose advantage. Lady Percy counters this with a different idea of pragmatic timeliness, that he should wait in Scotland to see how the rebellion goes without him, and join it when it begins to gain ground. Northumberland is persuaded once again to break his word, sink his honour, lose his good name.

ACT III, SCENE i

The King enters for the first time in the play. He is '*in his nightgown*'. We have already seen a character in partial night-attire – Northumberland in I.i. There, it signified the private man in his personal, domestic life. In addition, it suggested disorder since it was day and he was dressed for night.

Most obviously in the case of Northumberland, it was a sign of sickness – feigned sickness. Thus the coif also became a sign of deceit, of acting.

An actor has two identities, his real, private identity and his assumed, public identity. He is two people in one body. This, though, is a king. A king has two bodies: according to medieval legal theory, a king has an immortal, constitutional body (the ruling monarch's body, divinely ordained), and a mortal, human individual's body (in this case that of the man called Henry Bolingbroke). Just as we saw Northumberland caught between his public and private selves, so in this and subsequent scenes we see the King caught between *his* public and private selves, and increasingly under the strain of his inhabitation of his two bodies.

It is one o'clock at night. Henry *should* be in his nightgown. But he cannot sleep, he is up and active. Again, then, but in a quite different way, the nightgown signifies disorder and sickness. The insomniac King longs for sleep but is denied it. He has been up writing letters. Gradually, the play is exploring the ways in which words relate to things and to ideas, and how they operate in the world. A single word, 'Hotspur', was enough to inspire England's youth, but the word is that his father breaks his word (II.iii). And now we have an image of the King's word, as he communicates with his subjects.

That is his public word. But we also have an image of a king's private words, for this king has a soliloquy. Kings in their public bodies do not have soliloquies. They are attended and they are within their court. The private Henry is imagining what it is to be one of his subjects, able to sleep, comforted, reassured, revived by 'Nature's soft nurse' (6).

So, as in I.i and II.iii, we have a sick man, uneasy and in difficulties, frustrated in desire. When his counsellors enter he asks if they have read his letters. What they will have read is a 'reading' of the kingdom, a medical diagnosis of a sick patient:

> *you perceive the body of our kingdom*
> *How foul it is, what rank diseases grow,*
> *And with what danger, near the heart of it.*

(38–40)

The King regards his own sickness as deriving from his kingdom's sickness. Warwick diagnoses England's sickness as 'distemper' (41), i.e. it is out of temper, disordered. He prescribes the reimposition of order, i.e. strong, decisive government, as its cure. Only the King can cure the kingdom. In the King's terms this has to be read, 'Only the King can cure the King.'

23

But the King momentarily deflects the argument to a different topic and on to a different plane. He begins to analyse philosophically the nature of cosmic time.

Hastings has commented on the politics of time at I.iii.110: 'We are time's subjects.' Well, characters in plays have their being in theatrical time, but historical characters already inhabit the past as well – the actual past, and that part of it which is recorded, i.e. history. This play is classified as one of Shakespeare's history plays. It is about events in English history, but it is also about history itself, how it works, what laws it follows, whether or not it can be predicted.

In I.i, I.iii and II.iii, Shakespeare had invented for Northumberland and Scroop a theatrical time in which to debate the timing of their bid to be part of history. In this scene he invents for the King (already part of history and already, being guilty of a king's death, subject to the tyranny of the past) a theatrical time in which to delay his next move in historical time while he debates the ultimate nature of time itself.

> *O God, that one might read the book of fate,*
> *And see the revolution of the times*
> *Make mountains level, and the continent,*
> *Weary of solid firmness, melt itself*
> *Into the sea; and other times to see*
> *The beachy girdle of the ocean*
> *Too wide for Neptune's hips; how chance's mocks*
> *And changes fill the cup of alteration*
> *With divers liquors!*

(III.i.45–53)

The play has already established the fickleness of human beings, from Northumberland to Rumour's 'wavering multitude' (Induction, 19). The King now broadens the issue of inconstancy into a universal proposition – 'changes fill the cup of alteration' (III.i.52). The cup prostitutes itself to be used again and again by different drinkers, and we can never predict the nature of the next drink it will be holding. 'Liquor' brings together the imagery of liquids (with their constantly inconstant form) and of food and drink (which can both satisfy and turn the stomach). In the changing relations of land and sea we visualize first a swelling and then a shrivelling body. We also visualize both the Flood and the Apocalypse. Henry's times may be revolutionary but time itself is revolutionary, alteration merely brings us back to where we started from. Man is mocked.

The two earliest editions of the play were printed in 1600 (the Quarto edition) and 1623 (the text printed in the first Folio edition of Shakespeare's plays). P. H. Davison's New Penguin edition of 1977 is based primarily on the Quarto, but at this point he follows the Folio reading and omits three and a half lines from the Quarto text.

> *O, if this were seen,*
> *The happiest youth, viewing his progress through,*
> *What perils past, what crosses to ensue,*
> *Would shut the book and sit him down and die.*

They may be by Shakespeare, and they may not (see Davison, p. 225). They certainly continue the imagery of theatre and of reading. And, if accepted as authorial, they represent a low point in the King's spiritual health, as he proposes suicide as the revolutionary's solution to time's tyranny. If the sick kingdom was infected by the sick King, then the King's death is a cure-all.

Now, Shakespeare uses a dramatist's power to challenge both historical and theatrical time. Warwick proposes an analogy between history and the 'history in all men's lives' (76). According to him, the same developmental, evolutionary process operates in both time schemes – the macrocosmic and the microcosmic. He argues that seeds are sown in time and that the careful student of personal or natural history can prophesy 'the hatch and brood of time' (78–82). So Henry, desiring to prophesy the future of his kingdom, looks back into the seeds of time. He describes the political cooperation he had once received from Northumberland, by now the type of infidelity, alteration and the broken word. Not only is he rerunning the historical past, he is rerunning material Shakespeare has already dramatized in *Richard II*. (By an irony, Shakespeare is slightly unfaithful to his own earlier words, altering names, circumstances and speeches!) More interestingly Shakespeare allows Henry to present a *reading* of his own history.

For example, Henry denies that he had any intention of claiming Richard's throne when he returned to England from exile in 1399. But Shakespeare's earlier play had left this very much in doubt, and seemed to do so deliberately. The most damning aspect of the dramatization of events in *Richard II* is the fact that Henry returns from exile before he could possibly have the information that he has been disinherited by Richard – yet the reason he gives for his return is just that act of disinheritance. Furthermore, by the next act, Henry will be confessing

> *God knows, . . .*
> *By what by-paths and indirect crooked ways*
> *I met this crown*
>
> (*Henry IV Part Two*, IV.v.183–5)

Here, however, he disowns responsibility. It was, he says, necessity which 'so bowed the state/ That I and greatness were compelled to kiss' (69–70). A new abstract character has joined the cast list of those responsible for history – Necessity joins Fate, Chance and Time.

With the invocation of necessity, the argument moves from philosophy to pragmatism and to the kinds of calculation about the future which characterized the rebel scenes earlier in the play. The King begins to talk war with his counsellors. Shakespeare gives us the complementary situation to that of the rebels in I.iii. How many troops do the enemy possess? 50,000? But that is a calculation of the troops of Scroop and Northumberland combined and *we* know that Northumberland has withdrawn to Scotland. *We* have the ironical oversight of history, the divine perspective which makes mockery of men and encourages in them talk of Chance and Fate.

Warwick urges Henry to go to bed. He has been ill for two weeks now, and to be up at 1 a.m. is to be keeping 'unseasoned hours' (101 – an allusion, perhaps, to Ecclesiastes iii). Henry complies, taking counsel as a king should. But he goes to his bed to dream. What he desires of the future is a Crusade to Jerusalem, not a battle with Northumberland.

ACT IV, SCENE i

Gaultree Forest. At last the confrontation between rebel and government forces. In a move no doubt calculated as a snub (or 'gall', 89), Prince John sends Westmorland forward, refusing to dignify the rebel cause by negotiating with them in person. On the other side, rebel calculations have had mixed results. Mowbray has correctly estimated the number of government troops (30,000), but Northumberland has not turned up, writing that he cannot levy enough troops. Mowbray is forlorn: 'hopes . . . dash themselves to pieces' (17 – 18).

What we witness is not armed combat but the handover from rebel hands to government hands of a written document. The whole confrontation revolves around words, their power and their interpretation. When Westmorland attacks Scroop he does so primarily in the imagery of the word:

> *You, Lord Archbishop . . .*
> *Whose learning and good letters peace hath tutored,*
> *Whose white investments figure innocence . . .*

> *Wherefore do you so ill translate yourself*
> *Out of the speech of peace that bears such grace*
> *Into the harsh and boisterous tongue of war,*
> *Turning your books to graves, your ink to blood,*
> *Your pens to lances, and your tongue divine*
> *To a loud trumpet and a point [signal] of war?*

(41–52)

Scroop's answer is that he has 'justly weighed/ What wrongs our arms
may do, what wrongs we suffer' (67–8) and calculated that the latter
outweigh the former. Shakespeare has no interest in specifying the
nature of the rebels' grievances, preferring to represent them silently in
the written schedule Scroop gives Westmorland. Instead he stresses
Scroop's belief in historical timing:

> *We see which way the stream of time doth run*
> *And are enforced from our most quiet there*
> *By the rough torrent of occasion . . .*

(70–72)

Mowbray attempts to invoke personal family history and the old chivalric honour code (97–101, 111–27). But Westmorland believes that justice
is achieved through the process of history and that present political
realities are the only realities that matter. Prince John has offered to
read what they have written and, if persuaded of the justice of their
cause, he will agree to their demands.

Left alone, the rebels are divided. Scroop and Hastings are prepared
to trust the offer, Mowbray is not. They agree to meet Prince John at a
'just distance' between the two armies.

ACT IV, SCENE ii

The previous scene began with the entry of the rebel leaders '*with their
forces*'. Now we witness the entry of Prince John '*and his army*'. Political
conflict seems about to resolve into military conflict.

John speaks first, and at length. As prince this is in order, but the
rebels are at a disadvantage by acknowledging his right to do so. He
first reprimands Scroop for abandoning 'the holy text' (7), i.e. the Bible,
and replacing it with his schedule of grievances. This, he claims, is an
unholy transformation, a matter of 'Turning the word [the Word] to
sword' (10).

He then goes on to accuse the Archbishop of abusing his role as the
King's *shadow* (reflection, copy or representation).

27

> *That man that sits within a monarch's heart*
> *And ripens in the sunshine of his favour,*
> *Would he abuse the countenance of the king?*
> *Alack, what mischiefs might he set abroach*
> *In shadow of such greatness!*

(11–15)

Finally he turns to Scroop's role as God's shadow. Just as an archbishop mediates between the king and his people, so too does he mediate betwcen God and man. An archbishop, then, is like a book, or language itself, a mediating agent. He is, says John, like the Speaker in Parliament. (A speaker is an agent of language, and Parliament is the place where people *speak* – '*parler*'. The Speaker is speech writ large, the type of speech but, constitutionally speaking, he is the interface between king and Parliament.) An archbishop should be 'th'imagined voice of God himself' (19). In other words, like the actor in a mystery play playing the part of God.

If the King and the Archbishop both represent God on earth, they cannot clash without involving God in contradiction. To avoid the idea of conflicting systems of substitution, John must argue that Scroop has broken faith, broken his word. He is a deceiver, working 'Under the counterfeited zeal of God' (27), misleading 'The subjects of His substitute' (28).

Nevertheless, John agrees that there is substance to some of the grievances listed in Scroop's schedule. His father's representatives are to blame, having 'too lavishly/ Wrested his meaning and authority' (57–8), i.e. mistranslated his word. He picks his own words carefully. He promises that the rebels' griefs shall be 'redressed' (59).

Then he proposes a bit of theatre. First, the rebels must transform their soldiers from an army into an audience. Then, he and Scroop will act out a scene before them. It will be a dumb show involving two gestures: they will 'drink together friendly and embrace' (63). The soldiers will read this as 'restorèd love and amity' (65) and, like messengers, 'bear those tokens home' with them (64).

The rebels should be on their guard. Actors are deceivers and gestures can be misread. When John promises Scroop he will maintain his 'princely word for these redresses' (66), the word 'redress' remains ominously undefined.

Nevertheless they drink and, even before the gesture of drinking is completed, Hastings sends a message to his troops, the word of dismissal. John has led the rebels into a trap. The show of friendship in the drinking and intimacy of address ('coz') and the '*shouts within*' (signs of approval from the audience of this 'play' or, rather, travesty) are discordantly and perceptively undermined by Mowbray's sourness. When Westmorland drinks to the rebels' health, Mowbray comments ironically that the timing of the toast to health feels wrong to him, 'For I am on the sudden something ill' (80).

John then sends an order to dismiss his troops. Scroop, imagining the order is genuine, immediately dismisses his. And at *this* moment, the opportune time precisely – indicated by the change in direction of Westmorland's sentence, 'Good tidings, my lord Hastings – for the which/I . . .' (106–7) – Westmorland arrests the rebel leaders as traitors.

The rebels are defeated by their imaginations. High treason, according to Edward III's Act of 1350–51, includes the act of 'imagining' the death of the monarch. But the Prince has had the imagination to recognize the power of the imagination, imagining precisely how their imaginations will work. For their part, the rebels have miscalculated, unable to calculate for the calculations of the Prince.

Mowbray protests in the language of old-fashioned chivalry: 'Is this proceeding just and honourable?' (110). The scene's dramaturgy asserts that the answer must be 'no'. But Westmorland, rather than providing an answer, merely offers a complementary question: 'Is your assembly so?' (111). The answer to this short line would be no longer than the whole play. The meanings of justice and honour are functions of particular societies and rebels, by definition, reject the vocabulary of the societies they reject. Once a ruler acknowledges the justice of a rebel's cause, as Henry VI acknowledged the justice of York's cause in Shakespeare's *Henry VI Part Three*, the ruler's rule is over.

Scroop asks the next question: 'Will you thus break your faith?' (112). 'Faith' here means 'word', but coming from an archbishop it carries the implication of Christian faith as well. John's response is that he pawned (a commercial image involving an act of substitution) Scrope no faith. 'I promised you redress of these same grievances/ Whereof you did complain' (113–14). 'Redress' was his word, and he seems to be saying that it means 'answer', rather than 'agreement'. The rebels are dismissed contemptuously as shallow (118) and foolish (119).

John wraps up the scene efficiently, briskly and in neat, glib, resounding rhyming couplets – commence, hence; stray, today; death, breath. He completes the Archbishop's verse line for him and allows no one else to speak. He began the scene, and ends it. He is performing (115), but as an actor in someone else's play, someone else's war – 'God, and not we, hath safely fought today' (121).

ACT IV, SCENE iv

The King is in the Jerusalem Chamber, Westminster Abbey, at the centre of things spiritual as well as temporal. He enters first, speaks first, is seated surrounded by his sons and by his counsellors. All is well.

But all is not well. He is ill and (at least in Davison's opinion) enters *carried* in his chair. Each time we have seen him he has been sick. We think back to Northumberland once again, the first entry of the play, a father hobbling in on a crutch with a sick man's coif on his head.

The King opens by asserting that their destiny is in the hands of God. The sentiment that closed the previous scene in plot A is revived immediately here. The King is planning his crusade, indeed he is ready to go. Furthermore, he has chosen 'our substitutes in absence' (6). But not all his sons are in attendance. Where is Hal? Where is the man who will act for him when he is dead – the next of God's substitutes in England?

Henry begins to provide a character study of Hal: he is gracious if humoured, capable of pity and charitable generosity, but quick to fiery, hard and sharp anger. But having heard where Hal *is* – dining in London with Poins and company – the King's tone changes. He contemplates England's youth, life after his own death: 'I do shape/ In forms imaginary th'unguided days' (58–9). They will be 'rotten times' (60), days without constraint, days of disorder, dangerous days of 'decay' (66).

Warwick protests that the King 'looks beyond' Hal, i.e. exaggerates. He argues that Hal is engaged in his education, and that his subject of study is his subjects. He is engaged in the study of a foreign language (the assumption here is that there are two countries, and plot B is a foreign country to the inhabitants of plot A). It is in the nature of language that its vocabulary need not be used in its entirety, and that immodest words can be rejected 'in the perfectness of time' (74). Even the most immodest of his followers can provide a pattern, a measure, a copy, a shadow, whereby others can be measured.

Westmorland enters, promising health and peace. He offers the King a book, the official account of the victory of Gaultree Forest. Another messenger, another mediator, Harcourt brings more good news. At the battle of Bramham Moor, 1408 (history is compressed in this scene), Northumberland and Bardolph have been defeated. This too is written down and given as a 'packet' to the King to read (101).

But Fortune will 'never come with both hands full' (103). Rather, she will 'write her fair words still in foulest letters' (this is from the Folio). The King's sight fails, he feels giddy and he needs immediate help.

ACT IV, SCENE V

Hal makes his first entry in plot A. He arrives to find his father motionless in bed. He misreads what he sees, believing his father to be dead. So do we. He isn't. But neither we nor Hal know this. The irony is on us both. We are inevitably on Hal's side.

Hal looks at the crown which lies beside his father on the pillow. Hal thinks of it as his father's 'bedfellow' (23) and fears that death has 'divorced' (37) his father from it. It is as if the child were observing his parents in bed together, what Freud called the Primal Scene.

Hal soliloquizes, indulging the privilege of privacy which is denied a king. Yet he thinks he *is* a king and therefore no longer a private citizen. We are time's subjects, and our inheritance is beyond our control: 'This imperial crown/ . . . Derives *itself* to me' (42–4). Halfway through verse line 44 the stage direction reads '*He puts the crown on his head*'. Hal comments 'Lo where it sits' (44). *It* sits. The whole movement of the crown, from his father's pillow to his own head, seems an uninterrupted flow, part of the verse line – the *crown*'s action, not Hal's. The flow of succession and of history will not stop here: 'This lineal honour . . . from thee/ Will I to mine leave, as 'tis left to me' (47–8). Hal flows out of the room.

The King starts up from his swoon, calling out. Both Hal and we have been taken in. But another dramatic irony exists: the King does not know what *we* know – that Hal has been there with him, has taken the crown, was deceived by the King's sleep, and so on.

There is a different kind of irony in the fact that the King believes his crown to have been *stolen*. In the minds of his enemies, and to a degree within the mind of Henry himself, this accords with the events of 1399 when he usurped Richard II's throne. In Shakespeare's play of *Richard II*, Richard made much play of the idea that Bolingbroke was a thief, arranging a tableau in which they each held one side of the crown and Bolingbroke wrested it, as it were, from Richard's grip.

So Hal is here suddenly cast in the role of thief. But that is a role he has already had experience of. The robbery at Gadshill was one of the key events of the previous play, *Henry IV Part One*. And Hal's imprisonment by the Lord Chief Justice was meant to have followed from his arrest as a thief.

31

But Hal is also guilty of bad timing. He has certainly come at the wrong moment. But, in Henry's view, he has also been 'so hasty' (62), anticipating an event in history (his own succession) before its actual occurrence.

Further, he has made Henry ill and is out to kill him – 'This part [glossed by Davison as 'action', but maybe also suggesting the part he is playing] of his conjoins with my disease,/ And helps to end me' (65–6). It is not Death that has divorced Henry from his bedfellow, it is Hal, the Oedipal son 'killing' his father by imagining him to be dead and 'eloping' with the mother-figure, the crown. Hal is killing him because, like all sons, he is not only a rebel (67) but greedy for gold.

Henry's complaint against sons is revelatory in its imagery. In the first place, he proclaims himself a self-made man in the bourgeois-capitalist tradition, aligning himself with those fathers who labour to acquire gold (69, 73) and invest these 'engrossments' (74, 80). In the second place, he betrays his guilt at the nature of his engrossment: even if we accept the Folio's 'piled' (72) rather than the Quarto's 'pillèd' (pillaged), his pile was 'strange-achievèd' and 'cankered' (73), i.e. diseased.

However, Henry prefers to malign Hal as the friend of sickness, of Death (82). Yet Warwick argues for a different Hal, talking (84) of his cleansing, purifying tears and calling them 'kindly' (conscious of their kinship with the King) and his cheeks 'gentle' (not only upper-class but conscious of his *gens*, his race, his humanity, his part in human *kind*).

The King wants a private interview with Hal. It is the first interview of any kind between them, public or private, in the play and it takes the form of just five speeches. The first is merely a single line from Hal – 'I never thought to hear you speak again' (92). In so far as he speaks first it is a challenge to the authority of the man who is his father and his king. It is a line full of difficult emotion (shame mixed with concern) and in its brevity it implicitly expresses deference. It is followed by three immensely long speeches (forty-six, thirty-nine and forty-two lines respectively), a kind of formal debate between combatants but also a record of long-repressed feeling.

Henry's speech is full of disillusion. He interprets Hal's removal of his crown as 'hunger', i.e. political ambition. But he despises such ambition. For him, the throne, like the hollow crown and the journey to Jersualem, symbolizes the futility of desire in both men's lives. Disillusion manifests itself in cynicism laced with streaks of paranoid hysteria – he imagines Hal digging his father's grave himself, substituting the ritual of coronation (merry bells) for the ritual of funeral, collapsing time and destroying the social order.

Henry's fantasy becomes a kind of morality play, in which not only does Hal shift from the role of the innocent 'Youth' (97) to that of the Vice 'Vanity' (120) but, unlike all conventional morality plays, the Vices rather than the Virtues triumph. In the absence of order and constraint, foreign 'apes of idleness' (123), swearing, drinking and dancing as all Vices do, pour into England. The forces of disorder have taken over. The ruffian rules (and by 'ruffian' Henry may mean the Devil himself, since 'ruffin' is the Quarto's spelling, and Ruffin was a name for the Devil). So, too, does the Morality figure 'Riot' (line 136). Men have descended to the level of beasts. History runs backward. Time has gone into reverse.

It is Hal's turn to speak. But before he speaks he kneels, as a subject does before a king and a son before a father, and he gives back the crown. He invites his father to read these gestures, claiming there is identity between his outward form and the inner state of his soul. Here is no pretence, deceit, affectation (145). No acting. 'If I do feign/ O, let me in my present wildness die' (152–3). What does 'wildness' mean here? Is it the wild passionate state of the tearful, overwrought young man, is it the wilderness of sin or is it the wildness of his youth – the reputation that makes the world misread him? He swears he felt no joy or pride in wearing the crown for those few moments. Rather than hungering after the empty chair he talks of the crown as hungrily eating the body of the King (160). No 'rebel' spirit in him was active (172). He did not have 'the least affection [inclination, according to Davison; but could it not again be affectation?] of a welcome' for it (173). He refers to the way the poorest vassals kneel to the crown in awe and terror. Does he not kneel in this way now?

The King is persuaded of Hal's sincerity, even glad he took the crown, because it gave him the opportunity to explain himself. He calls him to his bedside in an intimate new tableau, reconciled, close and at the same level. In a reversal of roles the subject takes counsel from the King.

Henry describes his own acquisition of the crown in three very different ways – he actively snatched it (184, 189, 191), he passively 'met' it (185; compare Hal at lines 42–4), and he commercially 'purchased' it (199). However, with the King's death the crown 'falls upon' Hal (200), rather than being purchased, since he has it 'successively' (201), i.e. by succession.

Having acknowledged the complexity of his own position and asserted the simplicity of Hal's, Henry proposes a strategy for keeping the throne secure. The strategy is machiavellian in the strictest sense, pure rational practical politics: 'to busy giddy minds/ With foreign quarrels . . .' (213–14).

The scene has rehearsed the political and personal tensions active in Henry's life. It ends with their resolution. Henry has been reconciled with Hal, and Prince John enters, reminding us of the successful suppression of the northern rebellion and completing the gathering of Henry's family. More difficult to resolve is the moral pattern of Henry's life. It is in fact *impossible* to resolve, and this harsh fact is illuminated by Henry's wit in reading the significance of the setting in which he is to die: 'It hath been prophesied to me, many years,/ I should not die but in Jerusalem' (235–6), he remembers. In order to make the riddle come true, he asks to be carried back into the Jerusalem Chamber. He ends his life with a pun.

ACT V, SCENE ii

The old King is dead. The Lord Chief Justice says he fears 'all will be overturned' (19). His own future looks bleak – it was, after all, he who once put Hal in prison. Hal's brothers feel equally nervous. Should the court express what they believe and feel, or should they dissimulate and play a part? Clarence knows that the Lord Chief Justice will find it hard to pretend he admires Falstaff. The Lord Chief Justice prefers to die rather than pretend (6, 40).

The new King enters. Hal shows self-awareness and awareness of others in his opening words. First he calls attention to his new part, the new costume, the new title:

> *This new and gorgeous garment, majesty,*
> *Sits not so easy on me as you think.*

(44–5)

(Hal's 'gorgeous garment, majesty' suggests, as Davison points out, a separation between the two bodies of the king, the man and the office.)

Second, he calls attention to their fears (46). He reassures them, and simultaneously jokes. The joke distinguishes between English and foreign customs. He unites them, in other words, as Englishmen. It is part of the strategy his late father proposed he adopt. No longer will brother fight brother in civil war. He will unite the family of the kingdom. He will play *two* family roles at once: 'I'll be your father and

34

your brother too' (57). And he can do this because 'Harry's dead ...
But Harry lives', 'Harry Harry' succeeds (59–60, 49). The word-play
lightens the heavy mood, while affirming the legality of his constitutional position. He is king by succession. Yet, he says, they 'look
strangely' on him (63), i.e. treat him as if he were a foreigner, or they
foreigners.

Hal pretends to be angry at the old indignity – his 'rough' treatment
(70). The Lord Chief Justice replies that he acted as substitute for Hal's
father (73): 'The image of his power lay then in me' (74) and Hal
'pleasèd to forget my place,/ ... The image of the King whom I
presented' (77, 79), hitting the Lord Chief Justice and therefore his
father. The act of imprisonment was because Hal was 'an offender to
your father' (81). He appeals to Hal's imagination: suppose Hal were
his father (*Henry IV Part One* has already explored this possibility, at
II.iv, and events have now ensured that it has, in a constitutional sense,
come true), would he be prepared to let *his* son 'spurn at your most
royal image,/ And mock your workings in a second body?' (89–90). 'Be
now the father and propose a son,/ ... And then imagine me taking
your part,/ ... And, as you are a king, speak in your state/ What I have
done that misbecame my place' (92–100).

The blow Hal aimed at the Lord Chief Justice (or, as he puts it, at
the King), struck him in his 'very seat of judgement' (80). This means
both, as he sat in judgement on him in court, and also, on the temple
(the seat of thought and judgement). The play is much concerned with
two aspects of judgement – judicial thought and fine acts of judgement
in practical affairs (good timing, for example). So Hal's reply nicely
responds to both aspects. Editors have to decide whether to put a
comma before 'justice' in the next line (102). Davison does not. The line
therefore reads 'You are right justice, and you weigh this well', which
means 'You are the very embodiment of the judicial process, and perform your job well – as is evidenced by what you have so sensibly just
said.' If there *is* a comma before 'justice', he is merely saying 'I agree
with you, Lord Chief Justice, you have spoken with real judgement.'
The emphasis, not being on justice as an abstract concept, shifts to the
'weighing'.

The metaphor of *weighing* is pursued when, at line 103, Hal tells the
Lord Chief Justice that he is to continue to bear the balance (the scales
of justice). He also promises that the Lord Chief Justice will still bear
the sword (another symbol of justice), which he returns to him 'un-
stained' (114). The use of this symbol not only clarifies Hal's confidence
in his officer, it serves to remind us of Hal's own powers and duties.

Henry IV Part One concluded with the battle of Shrewsbury, where Hal demonstrated his loyalty and military prowess by putting the rebel Hotspur to the sword. *Henry V* will tell the story of Hal's military conquests abroad. But immediately after this interview with the Lord Chief Justice Hal will be crowned king and during the coronation service his profound responsibility for justice throughout the realm will be symbolized when he is presented with the Sword of Spiritual Justice.

Hal now proposes to the Lord Chief Justice that he should imagine a father–son reversal and the Lord Chief Justice should play out a new role:

> *. . . live to see a son of mine*
> *Offend you and obey you, as I did.*
> *So shall I live to speak my father's words:*
> *'Happy am I, that have a man so bold*
> *That dares do justice on my proper son;*
> *And not less happy, having such a son*
> *That would deliver up his greatness so*
> *Into the hands of justice.'*

(105–12)

The giving back of the sword was an imagined gesture. But Hal performs a real gesture now, before the court: 'There is my hand' (117). He glosses his gesture 'You shall be as a father to my youth' (118), for 'My father is gone wild into his grave' (123). What can he mean? Is he acknowledging his father's guilt? Perhaps such a meaning is there, a possibility raised, but immediately altered and replaced by Hal's own guilt: 'For in his tomb lie my affections' (124). Hal has buried his own wild youth with his father's death. A modern psychologist would argue that there is no cause for rebellion now the true source of rebellion, the authority-figure, is dead. Hal has moved into a new phase of life, leaving the Oedipal phase behind. What, though, are the 'affections' he refers to? Davison suggests some possibilities:

'Natural disposition' – that which will be modified by cultivation and civilizing influences – may be implied; or the reference may be to the Prince's (past) inclinations – the *riots*, excess, mentioned by Henry IV at IV.v.135 – or, simply, to lusts. (Penguin edition, p. 273)

But there seem to be other possible meanings as well. Why not the modern meaning, his strong, loving feelings for his father – the grave is a vault in which Hal has banked all his depth of feeling now; the sad self that remains is practical and political, coldly intent

> *To mock the expectation of the world,*
> *To frustrate prophecies, and to raze out*
> *Rotten opinion, who hath writ me down*
> *After my seeming.*

(126–9)

Finally, there is the possible meaning for 'affections' of *affectations*. Hal is going to stop acting a part now. The wild Hal was not the true Hal ('I know you all' – *Henry IV Part One*, I.ii.192). This, the new Hal, is the true Hal, not new at all. But a king's education is to try out disguises and roles, the stalking horses which enable him to observe his people and learn their language.

The morality play is over. Hal is Vanity no longer (130). His new form is *Majesty* (133). He turns to business, closing the scene, having the last word and getting things moving. He will call Parliament, he will rebuild, revive, the body politic (135–6). He will face peace *and* war. He calls the Lord Chief Justice 'father' (140) and himself 'Harry' (145). But unlike his real father's last words, Hal closes the scene with the word 'life' on his lips (145).

4. Summary of the Shape and Significance of Plot A

The shape of plot A is something which we, as readers, determine just as much as it was ever determined by Shakespeare. This is because it depends upon the decisions we take about how to read the plot. We may well, for example, wish to read it as the story of a particular character. It is not automatic that we would all agree about who that character should be but, if plot A is taken in isolation, the probability is that we would follow the suggestion provided by the play's title and look for the pattern of incidents which concern Henry IV.

But this is not a simple matter, for there are conventional roles which Henry plays out, each of which provides a different shape. Since Shakespeare presents the whole of his reign in *Richard II, Henry IV Part One* and *Henry IV Part Two*, it ought to be possible to trace the pattern of his reign as Shakespeare treats it. But it is an unquiet, troubled, fluctuating reign. Discord was there at its beginning (in the last two acts of *Richard II*), and continues through until his final hours. The triumph of his accession was marred by news of Aumerle's planned revolt and guilt over Richard II's death. The battle of Shrewsbury failed to quell rebellions. The outwitting of the rebels at Gaultree was followed immediately by Henry's death and Shakespeare makes no attempt to record any positive political or social achievements for the reign. Victory and defeat seem closely allied, and the overall impression is of the irony of events, encapsulated in the fact that Henry's ambition to reach Jerusalem is fulfilled in the letter (he dies in a room called 'Jerusalem') but not in the spirit (he has neither left England nor atoned for the murder of Richard).

If we regard Henry as a man who *aspired* to be king, then the shape of the play is merely the completion of a story which tells of his success, for he dies a king. If we regard him as a *usurper*, a criminal or traitor, the play is ambiguous in its significance – he is never forced to yield up the crown, except to his son and heir, but he cannot be said to *enjoy* the fruits of his usurpation.

If we think of him as a father to a prince, again the play provides an ambiguous message. Henry finally has the satisfaction of believing his son to be a worthy successor and a fit man to rule his country, but he has nevertheless had to endure the pain and indignity of knowing Hal to be a prince studiously generating the impression that he has no sense of his destiny and responsibilities.

Summary of the Shape and Significance of Plot A

Thus, each reading has to coexist with a contradictory reading which is equally valid. The structure and tone are deeply ironical, a complex mesh of narrative possibilities which resist satisfying resolution (creating a depressed, hollow, exhausted feeling) but which, at the crudest level, present the decline of a man obliged for his political success to rely upon the actions of his sons.

5. Plot B – the Falstaff Plot

Shakespeare's 'Alterations' of History in Plot B

Plot B is little dependent upon historical material and, although it includes characters such as Hal, the story of his youthful dissoluteness is legendary rather than historical and derives from such sources as *The Famous Victories of Henry the Fifth* (already discussed in Chapter 2, on p. 11). In the *The Famous Victories* a thief, Cuthbert Cutter, appears in court before the Lord Chief Justice accused of robbing a carrier at Gadshill. Hal argues that Cuthbert, being 'my man', has immunity from the law and, when his argument is resisted, assaults the Lord Chief Justice, giving him *'a boxe on the eare'*. But the latter arrests Hal and commits him to prison, thereby demonstrating that nobody, not even the heir to the throne, has immunity from the law of the land. There appears to be no substance to the story. There is certainly no mention in any official document of the Lord Chief Justice ever arresting the Prince, and during the period when Shakespeare would have us believe he was idling around Cheapside with Falstaff Hal was, in fact, extremely busy with political and military matters.

Falstaff's name has its origins in two historical figures. Sir John Fastolfe was a soldier during Henry VI's wars in France. Shakespeare makes him a character in his early play entitled *Henry VI Part One*. But Fastolfe had nothing to do with Henry VI's father. Rather, he was part of the retinue of Hal's brother, Clarence. Furthermore, although Fastolfe was accused of cowardice, Holinshed records that this was a slander.

In Part One of *Henry IV* Falstaff was originally known as 'Sir John Oldcastle'. Sir John Oldcastle, Lord Cobham, was a much respected soldier, well-liked by Hal. However, he was a supporter of the Lollards, followers of John Wyclif, who had propagated what were regarded as heretical beliefs and whose followers also came to be associated with revolutionary political beliefs. Oldcastle was arrested in 1410, escaped the following year when there was a Lollard uprising and was eventually burnt at the stake in 1417. Oldcastle's descendants clearly found it distasteful that Shakespeare should have given one of his most degenerate characters the name of their ancestor. During the printing of Part One, the name was changed to 'Falstaff'. (Fall-staff is not dissimilar to Shake-spear.)

Even so, the Epilogue to Part Two shows that the name was still a sensitive issue: we are promised that in the next play (i.e., *Henry V*) 'Falstaff shall die of a sweat, unless already 'a be killed with your hard opinions; for Oldcastle died martyr, and this is not the man' (Epilogue, 29–31).

Apart from his name, then, Falstaff is a creation of Shakespeare's imagination. If we feel that Hal's rejection of him weakens our affection or admiration for Hal, and if we feel that the imprisonment of Falstaff and the even more fictitious Shallow hardens our hearts against the Lord Chief Justice and makes us dislike Prince John more intensely, we need to remember two things. First of all, these events too are pure fiction. But secondly, they work to reveal Shakespeare's attitudes to the characters of Hal, the Lord Chief Justice and Prince John – all of whom have their origins in historical fact but all of whom have had their historical reality modified by the process of dramatization.

Plot B as Shakespeare Handles It

ACT I, SCENE ii

The introduction of Sir John Falstaff, already familiar to anyone who has read *Henry IV Part One*. The scene provides a minimal outline of both his past and his future. The Lord Chief Justice looks back to the final events of the previous play: 'Your day's service at Shrewsbury hath a little gilded over your night's exploit on Gad's Hill. You may thank th'unquiet time for your quiet o'erposting that action' (150–53). He then casts a prophetic shadow over the rest of this play: 'Wake not a sleeping wolf . . . You are as a candle, the better part burnt out' (156, 158–9).

Before these speeches, however – indeed, before anything at all is said – the audience witnesses a *tableau vivant*: the entry of the fat, limping (see line 248) man accompanied by a diminutive page who carries a sword. The comic-grotesque style of this tableau establishes the tone of plot B and the witty repartee of this scene, in which the page mocks his master, is characteristic of the comedies written by John Lyly (as well as countless comedies by other writers, where servants mock their masters – for example, Shakespeare's own earlier plays, *The Comedy of Errors* and *Love's Labour's Lost*). But each feature of the tableau is significant and contributes to the thematic structure of the play as a whole.

The gross size of the man signifies greed, animality, physicality, life. But his distinctive shape makes him immediately recognizable, not only within our culture (Falstaff is probably the best-known comic character in our literature) but within the world of the play. Indeed, he is already known from the preceding play in the history cycle, *Henry IV Part One*, where he proved himself to be a cheat and a coward but, by an irony, also gained the (utterly unjustifiable) reputation of being the man who killed the rebel Hotspur at the battle of Shrewsbury.

The man's limping gait signifies illness (confirmed immediately by the state of his urine). Later in the scene Falstaff feigns deafness, and then pretends concern for the Lord Chief Justice's health, saying he has heard he is sick, and alluding to his advancing age. He continues with his rudeness to his superior, chattering on about the King's ill health.

A sword is worn by a gentleman. In Falstaff's case it is also a sign of his newly acquired character of soldier-hero. We learn that, having acquired status through the Prince's gift of a page, Falstaff is now kitting himself out with new clothes and a horse, suitable to the courtier he aspires to be. When the Lord Chief Justice enters, Falstaff stands very much on his honour, as a knight and a soldier.

Falstaff advances a complex notion of himself. He is, he claims, both an inventor and a subject for other people's invention. 'Invention' here means *imagination* – a central topic in the play's potential meanings. Falstaff lives off and simultaneously feeds the imagination, his own and other people's: 'I am not only witty in myself, but the cause that wit is in other men' (9–10). Such a statement has its moral dimension, for it reveals him to be an embodiment of Vanity. But it is an endearing vanity that is not only hyperbolic but accommodates self-criticism and self-awareness. Furthermore, Falstaff comes up with a self-description, or rather a description of himself in company with his page, that is funny and vivid in its humour against self: 'I do here walk before thee like a sow that hath overwhelmed all her litter but one' (10–12). For all the comedy in this simile, further serious ideas about Falstaff's role in the play are provoked by his comparison of himself to an animal, a parent and a destroyer. His spiteful descriptions of Dommelton as a glutton (Dives) and as a perfidious and rejected counsellor (Achitophel) also have their ironies at his own expense. At the same time Shakespeare uses him as a social satirist, attacking the Puritans ('smoothy-pates' at 36–7). Once again this is double-edged: he acts as spokesman for the theatre's hatred of Puritanism, but his puerile humour (at line 191 he claims to have lost his voice while 'singing of anthems') undermines any claims he might have to moral superiority.

Falstaff makes jokes at the expense of his own physical shape and size in a way that reveals self-awareness – he is 'tallow', i.e. fat (160), he thinks of 'gravy' (164), he is not 'light' in weight (167–9). On the other hand, he conceives of himself as virtuous (170) and living in a second-rate age (171, 174), and he even talks of himself as being young ('we that are in the vaward of our youth', line 178).

This last claims astounds the Lord Chief Justice, and his response is a brutal piece of truth-telling:

Do you set down your name in the scroll of youth, that are written down old with all the characters of age? Have you not a moist eye, a dry hand, a yellow cheek, a white beard, a decreasing leg, an increasing belly? Is not your voice broken, your wind short, your chin double, your wit single, and every part about you blasted with antiquity?

(180–86)

Falstaff is insensible to the viciousness of this assault. He is so absurdly untroubled by it, and replies with such pleasure in his own power of invention, that one is persuaded to want to celebrate his spirit and witness his victory in the flyting match. There is something wonderful in the vision of innocence, and indeed the innocence itself, in what he claims:

My lord, I was born about three of the clock in the afternoon, with a white head, and something a round belly. For my voice, I have lost it with hallooing, and singing of anthems. To approve my youth further, I will not. The truth is, I am only old in judgement and understanding; and he that will caper with me for a thousand marks, let him lend me the money, and have at him!

(188–95)

Father and Child

He reveals how he likes to assume a fatherly relationship (at least in his imagination) with Hal: 'I have checked him for it, and the young lion repents' (197–8), but he follows this up with his other fantasy role, of being the naughty child laughing behind *his* father's back: '– (*aside*) marry, not in ashes and sackcloth, but in new silk and old sack' (198–9).

Somehow, the Lord Chief Justice's comment on the outrageousness of Falstaff's speech – 'Well, God send the Prince a better companion!' (200–201) – seems querulous and worthy only of mockery. And mockery is what it gets in a way, for Falstaff responds by suggesting that Hal is a drag, an irritating dependent – 'God send the companion a better prince! I cannot rid my hands of him' (202–3). Falstaff's skill is to redirect the challenge, never to respond to it directly. He and the Lord Chief Justice do not live in the same world. The Lord Chief Justice comes from plot A, Falstaff from plot B.

But to which plot does Hal belong? The Lord Chief Justice seems to assert that he belongs to plot A, and that that is where he is going to operate from now on: 'the King hath severed you and Prince Harry' (204–5). But, when he explains what form this severance is going to take, it transpires that it is *Falstaff* who is going to be taken up in the world of history and politics, the world of plot A: 'you are going with Lord John of Lancaster against the Archbishop and the Earl of Northumberland' (205–7). Falstaff's reply is a rag-bag of material. First there is bitterness that the Lord Chief Justice seems to have won a victory over him: 'Yea, I thank your pretty sweet wit for it' (208). Next, there is the assumption of the role of put-upon soldier who has to risk his life at the front while others look after themselves at home: 'you that kiss my lady Peace at home ... There is not a dangerous action can peep out his head but I am thrust upon it' (209–15). Then there is the assumption of the role of hero – Falstaff the braggart: earlier he was 'old in judgement' (192), now he is 'a good thing' made common by those who do not value him (217): 'I would to God my name were not so terrible to the enemy as it is' (219–20). (The irony here is that his name *is* terrible to the enemy – see Sir John Colevile of the Dale's surrender.) But 'I cannot last ever ...' (215–16). This leads him to the sudden grasping at the straw that reveals he has not forgotten the Lord Chief Justice's attack upon his old age: 'If ye will needs say I am an old man, you should give me rest' (218–19).

Finally, there is the promotion of the image, both fantasy and realistic, of the overweight man struggling through the labour and indignity of fighting on a hot day, sweating, thirsty, chafed by hot armour, preferring to be 'eaten to death with a rust' (210–21).

The Lord Chief Justice seems delighted to have got the advantage of Falstaff, for this speech suggests a man struggling to gain an advantage but driven into a form of self-pity. Falstaff's cheeky request for the loan of £1,000 is partly desperation too. The Lord Chief Justice makes a joke and goes off in good spirits. The confrontation is over, and round one has gone to the Lord Chief Justice.

Falstaff speaks sourly and contemptuously once the Lord Chief Justice is gone. He then falls to cursing age and sickness as they have afflicted him with gout and the pox. And he then turns to his impoverished state and describes that as a disease too. He sends his page off with begging letters to such dignitaries as Hal, and to 'Ursula' (Mrs Quickly perhaps?), believing that he can use his military service as a means to raising money if he is clever – his limp from the gout can be passed off as a wound from battle and he can claim a pension. Thus he 'will turn diseases to commodity' (250–51).

ACT II, SCENE i

We are in Mrs Quickly's Boar's Head tavern in Cheapside. She has begun a lawsuit against Falstaff for debt and has persuaded two officers of the watch to arrest him. But at the same time, she renders herself a figure of fun (though an endearing one) through her innocent use of sexual innuendo. It suggests she has been subject to sexual harassment and rape as well as financial trickery but she also seems to be revealing her willingness to give sexual favours. The portrait of Falstaff is similarly complicated by the assertion that the notorious coward 'will stab' (11–12) and, when he enters, he launches immediately into a fight with the officers.

The Lord Chief Justice appears with his men and takes command. The dramatic impact of the Lord Chief Justice's entry is to interrupt and end a violent, confused affray. This intervention of a different tone, like a cold draught suddenly let in when someone opens a window, is part reflected in, part the effect, of a shift into blank verse. Davison does not present the Lord Chief Justice's first speech as verse, but it could certainly be regarded as a line of blank verse:

> *What is the mátter? kéep the peáce here, hó!*
>
> (59–60)

Davison does, however, print the Lord Chief Justice's next four lines (63–66) as verse. Thus the worlds of plot A and plot B, of blank verse and prose, momentarily converge and clash.

Mrs Quickly explains to the Lord Chief Justice that Falstaff 'hath put all my substance into that fat belly of his' (72–3). Her delivery of her speech is described by Shakespeare as a 'tempest of exclamation' (79–80). She follows up with a speech of immense richness. It is not just in prose, but prose that is most persuasive in its natural colloquial quality – conveying at one and the same time the undisciplined nature of her mind (she rattles on, carried away by her vivid memory of the

45

events she is describing and the strength of feeling the memory provokes) and the almost tangible actuality of the world she is describing:

Thou didst swear to me upon a parcel-gilt goblet, sitting in my Dolphin chamber, at the round table, by a sea-coal fire, upon Wednesday in Wheeson week, when the Prince broke thy head for liking his father to a singing-man of Windsor, thou didst swear to me then, as I was washing thy wound, to marry me, and make me my lady thy wife. Canst thou deny it? Did not goodwife Keech the butcher's wife come in then and call me gossip Quickly? – coming in to borrow a mess of vinegar, telling us she had a good dish of prawns, whereby thou didst desire to eat some, whereby I told thee they were ill for a green wound?

(84–95)

And so on. This is in complete contrast with the texture of plot A. The world there is not described in local, material detail. The language is very largely metaphorical or abstract. Here, Mrs Quickly is almost entirely literal (only 'green' at the end being a metaphor, and certainly not an intentional metaphor on *her* part) and concrete.

Of course, her speech does other useful things too. We get an insight into Falstaff's methods here. He has been after her money not only by running up credit in her tavern but by promising to marry her and make her respectable: 'And didst thou not, when she was gone downstairs, desire me to be no more so familiarity with such poor people, saying that ere long they should call me madam?' (96–8). This emphasizes the theme of reputation, honour, public image, and it also suggests that Shakespeare is interested in satirizing the social pretensions of the aspiring middle class.

We also learn about Hal's relationship with Falstaff – that he is unprepared to listen to an attack upon his father's reputation and that he is capable of striking Falstaff as well as the Lord Chief Justice. In other words, Hal has hit two old men, two father-figures, on the head. (We also visualize a wounded Falstaff, with his head broken, with a green wound that needs washing.)

The 'singing-man' (88) allusion is problematic. As Davison points out it could imply that the King is useless and drunken. This makes no sense except that it nicely describes *Falstaff* and therefore links the two father-figures. But if it suggests a pretender to the throne and so someone who has doubtful authority for calling himself king, then Hal might well be sensitive on his father's behalf (and his father's honour would be at stake). It could, of course, be that his father's sexual honour is at stake, that a singing-man would be a eunuch. Falstaff's next speech indicates that he is perfectly happy to attack the sexual reputations of his superiors – he suggests that the Lord Chief Justice has fathered a bastard on Mrs Quickly – and at II.iv.278–9 he accuses both Hal and Poins of being bastard sons of the king.

The Lord Chief Justice moralizes sternly at Falstaff and seems to embody a firm but humane conception of Justice. He is perceptive – 'Sir John, I am well acquainted with your manner of wrenching the true cause the false way' (107–9) – aware of Falstaff's 'impudent sauciness', sympathetic to Mrs Quickly as the gullible victim of Falstaff's practices and analytical, measured and even witty in his judgements:

You have … made her serve your uses both in purse and in person … Pay her the debt you own her, and unpay the villainy you have done with her; the one you may do with sterling money and the other with current repentance.

(112–120)

This, we may think, is a different Lord Chief Justice from the man shown in I.ii. There he was somewhat irritating and absurd, and we wanted Falstaff to triumph over him. Now, as in any morality play, we have been manoeuvred into wanting to see Vice put down by what we recognize now as Virtue. In terms of his private war with the Lord Chief Justice, Falstaff believes himself to be on equal terms: 'This is the right fencing grace, my lord: tap for tap, and so part fair' (191–2). But his opponent dismisses him with contempt.

Again the world of plot A breaks in. The King and Hal are back from their engagements with the Welsh rebels, but 2,000 troops are marching north with Prince John to confront the northern rebels. Falstaff must go too, and plot B appears to be moving towards a military confrontation which will also be a marriage of both plots. Meanwhile, Falstaff comes to an agreement with Mrs Quickly. She will withdraw her action against him and lend him a further twenty nobles. In the interests of resolution, Falstaff appears to promise her marriage, the conventional goal in comedy.

ACT II, SCENE ii

This scene introduces Hal. We have heard of him a number of times – in the Induction (29); in I.i at lines 16, 109; in I.ii at lines 12, 19–28, 147, 200, 205, 241; in I.iii.83; and in II.i at line 133 – but the Hal we meet now comes as something of a surprise, because everything we have heard so far has suggested an active, lively man, whereas the note struck here is immediately one of lassitude, enervation, exhaustion (i.e. sickness): 'Before God, I am exceeding weary' (1). At the same time, we are told that Hal is aware that he should not be seen to be weary – it 'discolours the complexion of my greatness to acknowledge it' (4–5), i.e. he blushes to admit it. (However, Davison thinks that 'discolours the complexion of my greatness' means 'makes me pale.)'

This is not easy to interpret. It could well be that Shakespeare intends us to take this weariness very seriously. *Henry IV Part Two* was not composed much earlier than *Hamlet* and the prince of that play is originally characterized as being world-weary:

> *How weary, stale, flat and unprofitable*
> *Seem to me all the uses of this world!*
>
> (*Hamlet*, I.ii.133–4)

That the opening words of the scene should be as quoted above, and that the Prince's first image should be of a discoloured complexion, does seem to establish a spiritual sickness. Hal's speech at 9–26 is regarded as flippant by Poins, who comments

> *How ill it follows . . . you should talk so idly! Tell me, how many good young princes would do so, their fathers being so sick as yours at this time is?*
>
> (27–30)

In other words, Hal is sick to talk like this when his father is ill.

On the other hand, Hal has been fighting the Welsh rebels and has just arrived back in London after a hard campaign. He could be perfectly healthy and yet exhausted for a short time by his exploits. And he does not change his complexion because of weariness but at the thought that he should be known to be exhausted (and even then it is not a literal blush, presumably, but a metaphorical one). Above all, the tone of this scene is jocular, two young men being flippant together – before more serious thoughts break in.

Jocular as it is, Hal's conversation with Poins concerns the all-important issue of his reputation. He likes small beer, and he jokes, 'Doth it not show vilely in me to desire small beer?' (5–6). He knows that he is humbling himself to be spending his time with Poins (Poins's social standing never becomes clear, though): 'What a disgrace is it to me to remember thy name! Or to know thy face tomorrow!' (12–14).

This is ominous. It points forward to the time when Hal will no longer acknowledge the faces of his present friends.

Hal informs us that Poins plays tennis a great deal, and has fathered illegitimate children. The implication is that Hal lives the same life. He is certainly reputed to have squandered his youth playing tennis (see *Henry V*). But Shakespeare leaves the possibility open that Hal does *not* lead Poins's life, merely spends time with him and observes him. The argument will be advanced later in the play (IV.iv.67–78) that Hal is educating himself by mixing with the lower orders and the moral ne'er-do-wells.

In the preceding play, *Henry IV Part One*, Hal assures the audience in a soliloquy that he knows what he is doing, that he will abandon his companions and that he is uncontaminated by them and their vices. Here he rejects Poins's (joking) criticism that he is insensitive to his father's sickness, but the form of Hal's explanation of his behaviour is striking. He argues that, given his existing reputation, which is bad, 'it is not meet that I should be sad now my father is sick' (37–8). In other words, he is considering how things will *look*. It will appear that he is hypocritical.

At the same time, he tells Poins that his heart bleeds inwardly that his father is so sick (45). This is a moving declaration. But it is sandwiched between a harsh declaration of virtue and moral superiority ('thou thinkest me as far in the devil's book as thou and Falstaff, for obduracy and persistency. Let the end try the man', at lines 42–4), and a childish levelling of blame on to Poins for Hal's public behaviour ('keeping such vile company as thou art hath in reason taken from me all ostentation of sorrow', at lines 46–7). He seems unstable, being both coldly calculating and tensely emotional. His wish not to be thought a hypocrite (52) is complex, for he has become so self-conscious in his calculations that the very act of not behaving in a seemingly hypocritical manner is necessarily hypocritical itself.

We should note that when Poins accuses Hal, not only of being 'so much engraffed to Falstaff (58–9) but also of being 'so lewd' (58), Hal does not deny it. Once again Shakespeare seems to be deliberately providing contradictory information. We may wish to resolve it by choosing one reading of Hal at the expense of the other. Or we may say that Hal is a contradictory personality. Or we may say that there *are* two Hals, and Shakespeare refuses to unify them into one.

Bardolph comes, with Falstaff's Page, bearing a letter from Falstaff. There is a stretch of precocious Page humour in the Lyly fashion, largely at the expense of Bardolph's appearance (his red nose). We are clearly for a moment in the world of clowns and slapstick humour (like the fight at the opening of II.i). But because the theme is *blushing* (72) as well as sex and alcohol, Hal is again brought into focus.

Poins asks the Page how 'the martlemas' (Falstaff) is (95–6). The joke is instructive. Martinmas or the Feast of St Martin comes late in the year (11 November) and therefore suggests age. It is also the time when fattened cattle were slaughtered (just as Falstaff is going to be 'killed' at the end of the play) and feasted upon (just as fat Falstaff loves meat).

Falstaff's letter is an elaborate exercise in pomposity and verbosity. It also aspires to the status of art – imitating the laconic style of the Romans, but using three phrases or clauses in apposition whenever one would have done. It seems conscious of the importance of language as a projector of images; it is signed in three different ways because Falstaff believes there are three different audiences he has to consider in life: '. . . Jack Falstaff with my familiars, John with my brothers and sisters, and Sir John with all Europe' (125–7). What the Prince laughs at is the letter's pretensions, the effect it aims at, which is to impress and to advance Falstaff's reputation. But we sense that Falstaff is laughing too, at some level. And in particular, he is laughing when it comes to the meat of the letter, which is definitely brief but contains two appalling slices of cheek. First, he libels Poins: 'Be not too familiar with Poins, for he misuses thy favours so much that he swears thou art to marry his sister Nell' (120–22). The cheek lies in Falstaff accusing Poins of just the kind of unfounded claim that Falstaff would make – and does make to Shallow when he assures him that Hal intends to make Falstaff the next Lord Chief Justice. Then he slips in a piece of advice, 'Repent', almost as if he were his ghostly father confessor. The joke is reinforced in the words that follow that command – 'at idle times as thou mayst', i.e. repent when you have nothing better to do (122).

If Hal's philosophical observation 'Well, thus we play the fools with the time, and the spirits of the wise sit in the clouds and mock us' (135–7) is a strain of his serious nature, he quickly displaces it with a practical joke at Falstaff's expense. He and Poins will disguise themselves as drawers at the Boar's Head and be peeping Toms when Falstaff attempts the seduction of the prostitute, Doll Tearsheet, after his supper. Such a disguise is not only the act of an intriguer, a comic machiavel, not only the act of a practical joker, but a metamorphosis of man into beast. 'From a god to a bull? A heavy descension! It was Jove's case' (168–9). This is also a metamorphosis of the ruler into the subject: 'From a prince to a prentice? A low transformation' (169–70). It may be humbling, even humiliating, but 'the purpose must weigh with the folly . . .' (171). What, though, *is* the 'purpose'?

ACT II, SCENE iv

As with every scene in plot B, even II.ii, in which he is not present, this scene has Falstaff at its centre. His nature is becoming clear. He is the new man, risen into the circle of the court and full of ambition to rise further. His relations are careerist and commercial – Hal has given him a page, Mrs Quickly and Shallow will lend him money – and he has no time for the romantic idealism of the chivalric code which leads Hotspur to his death. He therefore expresses a post-feudal ethic and a vital dimension of Shakespeare's own society. And yet, because he is old, because he is associated with the youth that Hal outgrows before our eyes, and because he is another kind of romantic, a self-deceiving fantasizer, he is presented as belonging to an old, outmoded order. He lives in a continual present that is out of time, a time of wish-fulfilment, a time of the pleasure principle and the gratification of appetite. His fictional nature reinforces the truth that he lives in theatrical time and is therefore subject to a foreshortened time schedule (of three hours). Yet he is sick and old. Because of the processes of historical time and personal history, in 1413 he is going to be rejected. And then he is going to die.

Falstaff enters singing merrily, but his song, an old ballad about the young King Arthur's victories and splendour at court, ironically foreshadows Hal's ascendancy and Falstaff's consequent demise.

The set-up is degenerate and conflictual, an emblem of moral disorder. Quickly is supposedly Falstaff's fiancée but she seems happy enough to prepare Doll Tearsheet for his pleasure. Doll is the worse for drink and feeling sick. She talks of Falstaff's gluttony and accuses him of robbing her of her jewels. He denounces prostitutes for giving their clients the pox. As Quickly points out:

You two never meet but you fall to some discord. You are both, i'good truth, as rheumatic as two dry toasts; you cannot one bear with another's confirmities [i.e., infirmities].

(54–7)

Nevertheless, the commercial relations between Falstaff and the women cannot be disentangled from their affective relations. Quickly's intervention brings peace as Doll Tearsheet remembers that Falstaff is off to the wars and she may never see him again.

Pistol arrives. He is a social *type*, a swaggerer (69), i.e. a loud-mouthed hooligan picking fights with all and sundry (something like a modern skinhead, perhaps). But he is more than a type. He is distressingly violent and, abused by Doll as a pimp, a pickpocket and a bogus soldier, he threatens to kill her and causes an affray. But his imagination is also disturbingly active, even explosive, and fuelled by dramatic literature. He sees himself as the hero in a revenge play of the kind Elizabethan audiences might have seen in the new public playhouses in the city suburbs, not far from Cheapside. He is infected by the ranting rhetoric of stock Elizabethan tragic drama – and in places Shakespeare seems to be using him as a means to parody and satirize his contemporaries. Indeed, at lines 158–60, he borrows some lines from Marlowe (*2 Tamburlaine*, IV.iii.1–2). Meanwhile, we can see him as a quite different literary type, the braggart soldier (like Falstaff) in the dramatic tradition of Roman New Comedy.

Pistol's passions veer violently, carried away as he is by high-sounding language and quotation. The turbulence of his emotional life reinforces the disorder of the scene as a whole. One minute he is screaming for revenge, brandishing his sword, the next he is contemptuous of second-rate emotion, seeing himself as above such undignified behaviour as to 'fall foul for toys' (164). Either Pistol is drunk or else he is schizophrenic, like Edgar's persona of Poor Tom in *King Lear*. For all his nostalgia for the wonderful companionship of the past, everyone grows heartily sick of him, and despite his threatening gestures with his sword, he is driven out and down the stairs.

While wounding Pistol in the shoulder, Falstaff narrowly escapes being wounded himself in the belly and the groin – the seats of his twin passions, gluttony and sex. Doll is all over him now that he has protected her: he is honour and bravery personified. His reputation is once again enhanced and she continues by feeding his self-image as a man of action. But she also calls him, with almost maternal affection, a 'little tidy Bartholomew boar-pig' (226). This image of the pig fattened up for feasting reawakens the association of Falstaff with both food and sacrifice. When she asks 'when wilt thou leave fighting a-days, and foining a-nights, and begin to patch up thine old body for heaven?' (226–8), the implication is that he has never grown up, and now he is going to die.

*

At this poignant moment, when Falstaff is laid bare before us like a new-born baby or a sacrificial animal, Hal and Poins creep in to observe him. They have him at their mercy, all the more because Doll has exposed his weakness to us.

Falstaff asks her to stop talking of his mortality: 'Peace, good Doll, do not speak like a death's-head; do not bid me remember mine end' (229–30). Elizabethans sometimes kept a skull on their desks as a *memento mori* to remind them that all is vanity, everything dies. Falstaff's request is touching and an actor could make it tragic. On the other hand, comparing Doll to a talking skull is grotesque and unflattering, Falstaff may be thinking of the skull ring which prostitutes often wore, and the phrase 'mine end' could have sexual innuendo.

Doll asks Falstaff what he thinks of Hal and Poins. Falstaff falls into the trap, slandering them both. She asks the key question, the question we would like to ask ourselves, why does Hal hang out with Poins? (238) Falstaff says they share a schoolboy mentality. It seems to be true. Whoring, drinking and cursing were their conversation in II.ii, and now they are playing a practical joke on a broken-down old man. This is Falstaff the jester, telling the court home truths.

Hal may be amused, but his whispered commentary on Falstaff cruelly characterizes him as an elderly, withered, impotent knave, shaped like a wheel (250–58), and his question. 'Would not this knave of a wheel have his ears cut off?', refers to the penalty for defaming royalty. Hal has not forgotten his true social identity.

Falstaff begins to make love to Doll, asking for kisses, suspecting that she only pretends to love him, promising her gifts and bemoaning his advancing age: 'I am old, I am old' (265). Self-pity it may be, but Doll's response, 'I love thee better than I love e'er a scurvy young boy of them all' (266–7), generates a feeling of sincerity that deepens this sordid encounter into something touching and even reassuring. And yet, all the time, two scurvy young boys are undermining the whole mood by their silent presence at this intimate encounter of souls.

Falstaff wants a merry song and then bed with Doll. But when he says 'Come, it grows late' (270), one thinks of his life as much as of the time of day. A sobering thought arrests him: 'Thou'lt forget me when I am gone' (270–71). Doll protests she'll wait for him, and we realize she has taken this to mean that he is off to the wars. But the first reading must surely be that he is thinking of his death.

Hal and Poins step forward in their guise as drawers. Falstaff's surprise is as great as the actor makes it. Shakespeare merely provides him with a speech displaying quick wit – 'Ha! A bastard son of the King's? And art not thou Poins his brother?' Hal alludes to the complementary incident in *Henry IV Part One* (II.iv.261) when Falstaff claimed he knew all along that the highwayman who robbed him at Gadshill was the Prince in disguise. But this time Falstaff's defence is not that he knew Hal was overhearing him and that he has therefore not been tricked, but that he was not really maligning Hal at all: 'I dispraised him before the wicked [i.e. a prostitute] that the wicked might not fall in love with (*turning to Prince Henry*) thee ...' (314–15). He has been doing his duty as a loyal friend and subject, protecting the heir to the throne from the dangers of a temptress. He has been the Virtue in a morality play, not the Vice.

Hal dismisses this absurd rationalization as 'pure fear and entire cowardice' (321–2) and embarks on his own fantasy in which Doll, Mrs Quickly, Bardolph and the Page are figures of virtue. Falstaff rejoins by calling them all damned souls. The dialogue establishes a framework of moral categories – the wicked and the virtuous, the damned and the saved – and when Falstaff talks of Mrs Quickly's problems with the city fathers (she has broken the law by allowing meat to be eaten in her tavern during Lent), the categories are reinforced by the introduction of the concepts of the law and the church.

Simultaneously, Falstaff is talking about the division of the flesh and the spirit – 'His grace says that which his flesh rebels against' (345–6). He is also talking about meat and Lent (that period of fasting which culminates in Easter, the festival commemorating the sacrifice of Christ's body), which is ominous for him.

So, when the profundity (or is it shallowness?) of human contact is being explored, with ironic humour but also with pathos; when the Prince is most clearly acting a part and yet humbling himself; when the talk has drifted round to morality, to religion, to death, to sacrifice; and when a kind of camaraderie has been growing despite the talk of revenge and Quickly is greeting Hal like a prodigal son or a lost child in a romance – it is at *this* moment that a violent interruption takes place: 'Who knocks so loud at door?' (347).

Peto bursts in, and with him the world of plot A. The mood changes abruptly to high drama. The language shifts into verse. The outside world of public affairs and history and destiny blows in from the street into the fantasy world in which Hal is a pantler, Falstaff a sacrifical lamb, Doll a virtuous gentlewoman and Bardolph's face Lucifer's privy-kitchen.

> *The King your father is at Westminster,*
> *And there are twenty weak and wearied posts*
> *Come from the north; and as I came along*
> *I met and overtook a dozen captains,*
> *Bare-headed, sweating, knocking at the taverns,*
> *And asking every one for Sir John Falstaff.*

(350–55)

This news, and its new tone, has a double effect, galvanizing Hal into action and indicating that events and military/political realities are closing in on Falstaff and the world he represents. As Hal puts it

> *tempest of commotion, like the south*
> *Borne with black vapour, doth begin to melt*
> *And drop upon our bare unarméd heads.*

(358-60)

The imagery is of a natural event, a storm. This makes it seem inevitable and beyond human control. On the other hand, it is a 'commotion' and 'black' – it has some relation to disorder, and it is a judgement. Hal confesses, 'By heavens, Poins, I feel me much to blame' (356). In other words, the judgement is on *him*. He feels guilty because he has chosen 'So idly to profane the precious time' (357). He rushes out, pausing merely to say 'Falstaff, good night' (361). It seems peculiarly formal, ominous, prophetic. He won't be seeing Falstaff again, as it happens, until the final scene of the play, the scene when he is King Henry V and rejects his old companion, a scene set in the public streets and not in the fantasy world of the Boar's Head.

Falstaff bemoans the fact that he is to be denied 'the sweetest morsel of the night' (362–3). The image is of eating, but his association with night is equally significant, for night is the time for carousing – 'What! We have seen the seven stars!' (181–2) – for criminals, for dreams.

Further knocking (as in *Macbeth*). Falstaff's presence is demanded at court. Like a king, he is to be deprived of sleep because of his importance to the state.

As Falstaff is taken off into the night, Mistress Quickly thinks back over the twenty-nine years she has known him and she cannot recall an honester or truer-hearted man. Falstaff sends for Doll and she runs out crying. It is farcical, but it is also moving.

ACT III, SCENE ii

The play moves around the country, from Westminster to Cheapside, and then out of London and north to York. In this scene, we travel west to Gloucestershire. The setting is rustic, offering a pastoral alternative to the world of London, and a second alternative world to the court (the Boar's Head being the first alternative, as William Empson pointed out in *Some Versions of Pastoral*).

We meet two new characters, Shallow and Silence, both old men, both justices of the peace. They continue Shakespeare's exploration of age and time, and order and justice. Theirs is a sleepy, old-fashioned, timeless world. but Davy, the farm manager, has to work and he informs us of the business that has to be done day by day. The annual cycle and the weather provide the country with its own timetable and its own order.

Once again a scene opens with a man who is infirm: 'Come on, come on, come on! Give me your hand, sir, give me your hand, sir!' (1–2). It is morning, and the day that lies ahead seems to be there to be spent in desultory chat – Shallow catching up on the news of Silence's wife, daughter and son, and then both men reminiscing about college days at Clement's Inn in London. Their memories are of wild times such as Hal and Poins seem to be having nowadays: 'they will talk of mad Shallow yet' (13–14); 'You were called "lusty Shallow"' (15); 'I would have done anything indeed too, and roundly too' (16–17); 'you had not . . . such swinge-bucklers [swash-bucklers] in all the Inns o' Court again. And . . . we knew where the bona-robas [best prostitutes] were, and had the best of them all at commandment' (20–23).

It transpires that they were near-contemporaries of Falstaff, for 'Then was Jack Falstaff, now Sir John, a boy, and page to Thomas Mowbray, Duke of Norfolk' (23–5). We are reminded instantly of *Richard II*, where Thomas Mowbray (whose son features as one of the rebels in this play) was the immediate cause of Bolingbroke's banishment – the banishment which provoked Bolingbroke to challenge King Richard II's right to deprive him of his title as the heir to the property of John of Gaunt (another figure from the past whom Shallow and Silence vividly remember). Whether this Mowbray is that Mowbray, or one from an earlier generation, hardly matters. The important thing is that our attention is directed at an outworn world, the world pre-Henry IV, i.e. pre-usurpation, the world indeed of the present King's father. The play thus spans the relations between *three* generations, not just two.

Shallow is in love with his youthful self, and no doubt he exaggerates his account of it. But there is enjoyment in his enjoyment of it. His

mind is disorderly in so far as it slips from ancient memories to philosophical meditations to immediate local concerns. Thus

> *the very same day did I fight with one Samson Stockfish, a fruiterer, behind Gray's*
> *Inn. Jesu, Jesu, the mad days that I have spent! And to see how many of my old*
> *acquaintance are dead! . . . Death, as the Psalmist saith, is certain to all; all shall*
> *die. How a good yoke of bullocks at Stamford fair?*

(30–37)

As with Mrs Quickly's mind and language, the texture of Shallow's
speeches is concrete and vital with the detail of real life. And the
psychological realism in the movements of Shallow's mind reinforces
that impression.

But the topic of death, once raised, becomes insistent.

SHA.   *Death is certain. Is old Double of your town living yet?*
SIL.   *Dead, sir.*
SHA.   *Jesu, Jesu, dead! 'A drew a good bow, and dead! . . . Dead! . . . And is old*
        Double dead?

(39–51)

And this threnody, rhythmic and harshly realistic, is juxtaposed with
the inquiry 'How a good yoke of bullocks at Stamford fair? . . . How a
score of ewes now?' (37–48) – equally rhythmic and realistic.

Shallow conceives of himself as 'a poor esquire of this county' (56–
7) and Falstaff as a great man from London. But Shakespeare uses
Falstaff to satirize a scandal of his own day, the corrupt recruiting
officer who accepts bribes from able-bodied men and enlists 'tattered
prodigals' in their place. Each of the five recruits Falstaff interviews
(Shallow claims he has half a dozen, but Falstaff doesn't seem to notice
he is one short) is a figure of fun. It is something of a music-hall
routine, this parade of grotesques. But it is also a parody of those
archetypal stories (such as *The Merchant of Venice* or *King Lear*) in
which a choice has to be made between contenders for a prize. The only
thing here is that the prize is death and Falstaff's choices are merely commercial.

Bullcalf roars because of 'A whoreson cold, sir, a cough, sir, which I
caught with ringing in the King's affairs upon his coronation day, sir'
(178–80). But that was fourteen years ago. Some cold to have caught!
Shallow is thinking back much further, fifty-five years in fact, to the
days of his and Falstaff's youth. It is early morning now, but what he
remembers is a night, a merry night with Jane Nightwork in the Wind-
mill in Saint George's Field in Southwark (i.e. not far from the theatres

in Shakespeare's day). As well as the nostalgia, there is, once again, the knowledge that time not only passes but alters everything.

SHA. *... Doth she hold her own well?*
FAL. *Old, old, Master Shallow.*
SHA. *Nay, she must be old, she cannot choose but be old, certain she's old ...*

(200–203)

So when Falstaff reminisces 'We have heard the chimes at midnight' (209) he is not only recalling the past, a night of revelry, but the breaking into that night of the brute fact of the passage of time. Since midnight is twelve o'clock, the last in a sequence of hours, the death of night seems also to be a terminal time. It is as if Falstaff had not really understood but nevertheless been conscious that night of the chimes of the church clock. Now, in retrospect, that memory can be interpreted as prophetic. Such alteration also typifies the nature of time.

Part of the pleasure of this scene is the speed and economy with which Shakespeare creates each of the characters who make up the recruits – sometimes merely by giving them a name (Wart, Mouldy, Feeble), sometimes by the combination of name and behaviour. Bullcalf's reasons for not being recruited are confused – as he is, presumably. But Mouldy's are quite affecting – his old dame has nobody else to 'do anything about her' (224–5). Feeble, on the other hand, does not try to evade the press, being fatalistic: 'a man can die but once ... An't be my destiny, so; an't be not, so ... he that dies this year is quit for the next' (228–32). This is like Hamlet's stoicism at the point when he is back from England and facing the duel with Laertes. Feeble's loyalty is to his king ('No man's too good to serve's prince', at lines 230–31) and to his God ('we owe God a death', line 229 – punning on the Elizabethan pronunciation of death/debt). Such innocent loyalty contrasts cruelly with the self-interest of Falstaff, who is happy to send this man to his death if he does not offer money to be kept alive.

Self-interest is not restricted to Falstaff. Shallow is not only sycophantic –

Ha, ha, ha! Most excellent, i'faith! Things that are mouldy lack use! Very singular good, in faith, well said, Sir John, very well said

(107–9)

– but he is using Falstaff as much as Falstaff is using him:

At your return, visit my house; let our old acquaintance be renewed. Peradventure I will with ye to the court.

(284–6)

Falstaff, for his part, is full of playfulness and seeming good humour, genially indulging Shallow's senilities. But left alone at line 291, his tone changes. He becomes malevolent and malicious and mean, full of contempt for Shallow. His pun on Silence's name at lines 279–80, 'I will not use many words with you', was a pleasantry; now, however, behind Shallow's back he comments, 'I do see the bottom of Justice Shallow' (291–2). By this he means that Shallow's recollections of the past are a fabrication –

how subject we old men are to this vice of lying! This same starved justice hath done nothing but prate to me of the wildness of his youth . . .

(the phrase is significant, of course, picking up the theme of Hal's wildness)

. . . and every third word a lie . . .

(292–6)

What is remarkable is that Falstaff describes himself (*a*) as an old man and (*b*) as a liar. This is a soliloquy and, like Richard III or Iago, Falstaff tells *us* the truth where he would never admit it to any character in the play. Just like Rumour, the admission that he is a liar could involve us in a logical contradiction. The phrase 'this vice of lying' encourages a reading of the Falstaff world in terms of the morality play structure: his soliloquy is Vice-like in its taking the audience into his confidence and its declaration of intention, 'I will fetch off these justices' (291). It is as if (like Iago) he were searching for a motive to explain his own behaviour. His attitude to Shallow is envious – 'And now is this Vice's dagger become a squire . . . And now has he land and beefs' (308 – 16) – and he despises him for his youthful insipidity, and his bragging and lying. But he also attempts to justify his own predatory intentions by appealing to the law of Nature –

If the young dace be a bait for the old pike, I see no reason in the law of nature but I may snap at him.

(318–20)

The weak were born to be preyed upon by the strong. In a sense Falstaff's explanation is sufficient, for there is nothing to explain Falstaff's nature except the fact of his behaviour. This *is* how he is. It's not an attractive side of Falstaff. His imaginative description of Shallow as being so thin that

you might have thrust him and all his apparel into an eel-skin – the case of a treble hautboy was a mansion for him, a court

(313–16)

and his earlier image.

When 'a was naked, he was for all the world like a forked radish, with a head fantastically carved upon it with a knife

(299–301)

are delightful in their use of the homely and the fanciful, but they are subject to the more forceful impression left by the harsh, selfish intrigue that begins and ends the speech.

Falstaff's final sentiment, 'Let time shape, and there an end' (320–21), is grim as a reflection of Falstaff's plan, but ironical in that it looks forward to Falstaff's own demise and looks back and forth over the whole history of the political figures in these plays.

ACT IV, SCENE iii

'Alarum. Excursions.' These are off-stage trumpet calls and soldiers' on-stage sorties – the only genuine military action of the play. This is in contrast with *Henry IV Part One*, *Henry V*, *Henry VI Parts One*, *Two and Three*, and *Richard III*, in all of which scenes of battle provide major structural features. *Henry IV Part Two* is not about armed conflict. It is about peace, but a strangely handled peace, and a peace that is uneasy and in many ways unconvincing. In this respect it is like *Richard II*, where there is plenty of talk of conflict, both personal combat and fully-fledged war, but confrontation, victory and defeat are effected in words and ritualized actions such as disinheritance and abdication.

The scene as a whole is about Falstaff and his belly. Colevile surrenders to him because Falstaff's fame, like his belly, goes before him. Fame has come his way because of his reputation as the killer of Hotspur. Colevile kneels, reflecting both the force of that reputation and the collapse of the rebels' opposition as a whole – a brave warrior kneeling to a fraud. 'Had they been ruled by me,' says Colevile of his 'betters' in

60

the rebel army, 'You should have won them dearer than you have' (65–6).

Falstaff wishes to make an emblem of this tableau, he with his fat belly standing over the fallen enemy: 'I have a whole school of tongues in this belly of mine, and not a tongue of them all speaks any other word but my name' (18–20). His name is broadcast far and wide, and his belly is as famous as his name. Indeed, his figure operates like a word in a universal language. Falstaff is here not only boasting but making fun of himself at the same time: 'my womb, my womb, my womb undoes me' (22). W.H. Auden pointed out that Falstaff, being a fat man, 'looks like a cross between a very young child and a pregnant mother' ('The Prince's Dog', in G. K. Hunter, ed., *Shakespeare: 'Henry IV Parts 1 and 2'*, 1970, p. 200). When he complains that his womb undoes him it is almost as if, being simultaneously his own mother and his own child, he were cursing the womb that gave him birth.

This dark despair is highly suggestive. Is it prophetic of the end to come? Was he born to be the sacrificial victim to Hal's ambition or vocation as prince? Or is it part of a self-destructive urge in Falstaff that coexists with his cheek, his wit, his vital energy and pleasure principle?

Prince John's tone is practical, abrupt, contemptuous of Falstaff. He speaks in blank verse, but Falstaff sticks obstinately to prose and to his own ambiguous position – calling attention to his size, yet boasting of his military prowess. It is very funny, shifting as it does from attitude to attitude (hurt feelings, philosophical observation, outrageous self-congratulation, over-the-top arrogance and exaggerated rhetoric). Having associated his triumph over Colevile with Caesar's Pontic triumph, Falstaff wants to be immortalized himself in art, so that his fame is the further extended: 'I will have it in a particular ballad ... with mine own picture on the top on't, Colevile kissing my foot' (46–8). If this is achieved, he fantasizes, John and Blunt will 'show like gilt two-pences to me, and I in the clear sky of fame o'ershine you as much as the full moon doth the cinders of the element [the stars], which show like pins' heads to her' (49–52).

Left alone with his belly, Falstaff delivers himself of a bellyful of prose – this time abusive and contemptuous of his general (compare III.ii.291–321, where he similarly turned on his host, Shallow). But much of the speech is about alcohol (a frequent cause, as Auden points out, of big bellies). Falstaff's complaint is that John's lack of wit, virility, courage and humanity is a consequence of his taste for '*thin drink*' (90). Hal, by contrast, has the good sense to drink 'good and good store of fertile sherris' (118–19), which has the effect on the '*lean*, sterile and bare land' of his inherited cold blood of having 'manured, husbanded, and tilled' it (116–17). Hal's education has been not in books but in bottles, and 'skill in the weapon is nothing without sack, for that sets it a-work, and learning a mere hoard of gold kept by a devil, till sack commences it and sets it in act and use' (111–14). Learning and valour are the attributes of the gentleman, the courtier, the prince. Hal is aspiring to be king, Falstaff is aspiring to be a gentleman at court.

The speech concerns food as well as drink. By aligning himself with red-bloodedness – cold blood is 'white and pale' (103) whereas hot blood 'illumineth the face' (106) – and against 'many fish meals' (91), i.e. cold-blooded creatures, Falstaff is orienting himself not just with fatness as opposed to thinness but, in the tradition of the springtime street festival of Mardi Gras, with fat-bellied 'Carnival', the lover of meat, as against 'Lent', the lover of fish.*

The scene ends with Falstaff's resolve to make his second visit to Shallow and relieve him of some money. Having delivered himself of so much language, Falstaff's imagery is of sealing a letter, Shallow being the letter. Falstaff is nearly at the climax of his fortunes now. His reputation is advanced and his next victim seems about to succumb to his wiles.

ACT V, SCENE i

Falstaff is back in Gloucestershire. Last time it was early morning, now it is evening and Shallow is begging his guest to spend the night. Davy is trying to get decisions out of Shallow in order to run the farm ('shall we sow the hade land with wheat?', line 12) and conduct the business of justice of peace ('I beseech you, sir, to countenance William Visor of Woncot against Clement Perkes o'th'Hill', lines 33–4).

The real world of country life is documented in the detail of Davy's concerns – the costs ('the smith's note for shoeing and plough-irons', lines 15–16; 'a new link to the bucket must needs be had', lines 19–20,

---

*There are exceptions to this (we know from Mrs Quickly that, when Hal had wounded Falstaff in the head 'upon Wednesday in Wheeson week' and he was bleeding, he had expressed the desire to eat prawns, at II.i.86–94) but almost all the descriptions of Falstaff conjure up associations with meat.

whether 'to stop any of William's wages, about the sack he lost at Hinckley fair', lines 20–21), the food he must order the cook to prepare (pigeons, a couple of short-legged hens, a joint of mutton, 'and any pretty little tiny kickshaws', lines 22–4), his horror at the unhygienic state of the new guests ('they have marvellous foul linen', lines 29–30) and his need to watch them carefully ('for they are arrant knaves', line 28).

Breaking into all this Chekhovian detail are the counter-currents (again Chekhovian) of the deeper preoccupations of master and servant. Shallow admits that his hospitality to Falstaff is disguised self-interest: 'I will use him well; a friend i'th'court is better than a penny in purse' (26–7).

Davy feels that there is a clash between the principle of legal justice and the principle of friendship to William Visor (there are three Williams in this scene):

I grant your worship that he is a knave, sir; but yet God forbid, sir, but a knave should have some countenance at his friend's request . . . The knave is mine honest friend, sir . . .

(37–44)

Both these issues – the deep strata of (a) self-interest and (b) loyalty to friends – will surface dramatically in the famous rejection of Falstaff, where both parties can be accused of self-interest, and the ties of friendship seem to be severed by one party at the expense of the other. Both here and there the more abstract ideals (of hospitality and justice, for example) are modified, though not exploded, by our knowledge of these profound commitments.

Falstaff agrees to stay to supper, and is once again left alone to soliloquize. His theme is, ironically enough, 'let men take heed of their company' (70–71). Very soon Hal will act upon such advice. For the moment Falstaff's theory, that 'either wise bearing or ignorant carriage is caught, as men take diseases' (68–70), derives from his observation of the relationship between Shallow and Davy. He finds the way they work together 'wonderful' (58). His sarcasm reflects his contempt for what he sees as the folly and self-delusion of Shallow – 'If I had a suit . . . to his men, I would curry with Master Shallow that no man could better command his servants' (64–8) – for Shallow's commands are certainly followed but only amidst the mêlée of Davy's multiple responses. And Falstaff is also contemptuous of Davy for retaining the respect the servant has for his master despite the servant's notion that *he* is running the farm and the local court. Davison argues that Shallow and Davy's relationship is humane and preferable to both Falstaff's theory and his practice (this view is partly dependent on a particular reading of Shallow's reassurance to Davy about William Visor: 'he shall have no wrong', at line 46, which he takes to mean he shall be fairly treated, rather than the corrupt reassurance, he shall win his case).

Falstaff throws in a little satire of the court, mocking the ephemerality of fashion and the sloth of the legal profession. But primarily he sees himself as the court satirist of country manners (like Touchstone in *As You Like It*). For all his wit – as in the brilliance of the closing image, in which the creases of laughter are compared to 'a wet cloak ill laid up' – events will soon be outwitting Falstaff. It is with ill-founded complacency that he looks forward to retelling his Gloucestershire adventures to the Prince in a few days' time.

ACT V, SCENE iii

They have supped and are exploring Shallow's orchard. Shallow and, above all, Silence have drunk too much. The latter sings five songs, having been virtually silent before this scene. These drinking songs celebrate human concourse, companionship, love, maleness and virility. There are sixteen references to merriment in sixty-one lines (18–79). Meanwhile Davy is plying them all, including Bardolph and the page, with food – 'a last year's pippin ... a dish of caraways ... a dish of leather-coats' (2, 3, 40) – as well as drink. This is the most harmonious and warmest scene of the whole play. Falstaff may be lying, but his compliments to Shallow seem heartening –

'Fore God, you have here a goodly dwelling, and a rich ... This Davy serves you for good uses ... There's a merry heart, good Master Silence!

(5, 6, 10, 23)

When he calls it a rich dwelling, and Shallow replies 'Barren, barren, barren; beggars all, beggars all' (7–8), it is clearly susceptible of a reading that reveals them both to be thinking primarily in financial terms. But a more innocent reading is just as allowable in which Falstaff is merely impressed by the good life he's been leading with them, and Shallow is conventionally or even genuinely persuaded of his humble lifestyle and relative poverty. Davy's 'I hope to see London once ere I die' (59) is an entirely innocent version of Shallow's earlier articulated desire to get to court. Bardolph's reply to Shallow's opinion that, if he got to London, Davy would stick by Bardolph – i.e. drink with him – is probably ironical ('And I'll stick by him, sir', line 67, i.e. I'll take advantage of this innocent abroad), but might just mean I'll be a good friend to him in London.

For the second time in the play, the holiday mood which Falstaff always works for is interrupted by a knock at the door (see II.iv.347). The last words before the knock are Shallow's: 'Why, there spoke a king. Lack nothing! Be merry!' (68–9). It is Pistol with the news from London: 'Sweet knight, thou art now one of the greatest men in this realm' (87–8). Falstaff's first question to him had been 'what wind blew you hither, Pistol?' (85), as if he were a natural force, and indeed he does represent a natural force, Death. When Pistol picks up Silence's joke about goodman Puff of Barson, 'Puff?/ Puff i'thy teeth . . .' (91–2), it is as if he were reinforcing the idea that he was that wind of change – 'Not the ill wind which blows no man to good' (86).

Pistol embarks upon his verses, further reinforcing that idea of change, proclaiming 'lucky joys,/ And golden times' – a romantic, pastoral vision – 'and happy news of price', a time of financial happiness to come (95–6). His imagination carries him to 'Africa and golden joys' (100) and then to Mount Helicon in mythological Greece. Falstaff fuels the fantasy by invoking the world of romances and folk ballads (101–2). Within this complex of literary allusions, and therefore of imaginative escape, Pistol is delivered (97) of the news that they are subjects now of Henry V.

FAL.   *What, is the old King dead?*
PIS.   *As nail in door! The things I speak are just.*

(119–20)

Surely this is the ill wind? Surely the knocking on the door was ominous, as it had been in II.iv? Surely, this is not the stuff of pastoral romantic joy? But no.

BAR.   *O joyful day! . . .*
PIS.   *What, I do bring good news?*
FAL.   *. . . O sweet Pistol!*

(124–30)

The first thing that is established by Pistol's news is the constitutional fact of the transfer of power from one man to another – from Henry to Hal. But this transference is seamless. According to the theory of the king's two bodies, the king never dies, or at least his constitutional body never dies. There is always a monarch ruling. The mortal body of the individual who occupies the constitutional position of monarch may die, but at that instant the constitutional body is occupied by the new incumbent. Hence, the riddle:

SHA. *I am, sir, under the King, in some authority.*
PIS. *Under which king . . . ?*

Shallow's authority as JP derives from Henry IV. He therefore answers 'Under King Harry'. But Pistol rightly asks *which* Harry, 'the Fourth, or Fifth?' It is a double riddle. Which king, which Harry? And he makes a pun out of Shallow's reply, 'Harry the *Fourth*', 'A *foutre* for thine office!' (115). Shallow is no longer a JP! So, for him, it should be *bad* news.

Pistol tells Falstaff 'thy tender lambkin now is King' (116). The suggestion is that Falstaff's child (not Bolingbroke's) has succeeded to the throne, that Falstaff is the father. The further suggestion is that Hal is a lamb. A sacrificial lamb, perhaps? A tender meal? But 'Harry the Fifth's the *man*' (117), not the child, and not the lamb, any more.

Shallow may have lost a job, but Falstaff has gained one – or so he thinks. The Lord Chief Justice's job is surely his, and with that position at court he can promise Shallow any job he wants (121–3), and Pistol too, and Bardolph. Falstaff is 'fortune's steward' (128–9). They are all made men and will ride all night, commandeering any man's horses (for on the King's business they have such a right). Falstaff believes that 'the young King is sick for me' (133). He has misjudged what is happening: Hal is sick *of* him, not sick *for* him.

Pistol's closing lines are therefore highly ironical. The vultures will seize on them, the old life has gone, the new days will be far from pleasant, and the lover's lament for lost freedom reflects the fate of Falstaff in the Fleet prison.

ACT V, SCENE iv

An ugly scene in or near the Boar's Head some time later. A man has died as a result of a beating he suffered at the hands of Pistol, Doll and Quickly, and Doll has been the cause of at least one more killing. The beadles are trying to arrest Doll and Quickly, and the prospect for Doll is to be whipped through the streets as a prostitute. Doll is pretending to be pregnant to escape her punishment, Quickly is trying to fight off the beadles and Doll is abusing them, calling one of them (a thin one) 'Goodman death, goodman bones!' (28), while Quickly wishes the fat Falstaff were there to defend them. Birth and death, crime and punishment, deceit and justice, male oppression of women and female oppression of men. This brutal, sordid, almost comic-grotesque scene focuses in a clash of elements the profoundest themes, a sickening policing of the streets, and a counter-current to the imaginative hopes of the preceding scene.

ACT V, SCENE V

The confusion and inglorious nature of the preceding scene is followed by the pageantry of a coronation procession in the streets. These streets have been cleared up by the beadles and are newly strewn with rushes. Trumpet calls proclaim formality and ritual. We see the new King on his way to be crowned.

Falstaff is much concerned with appearances, calling on his companions to 'mark' (7) and read the signs and gestures, arranging who will stand where, regretting the lack of new liveries, preferring to display the urgency of his desire to see Hal – which is presented as 'this poor show' (13), but which seems, by the rhythms employed and the insistence of the attempt to clarify the situation ('It shows . . . As it were . . . as if', at lines 16–26), to be genuine and authentic. When Pistol, in a speech which might come from a revenge tragedy, urges Falstaff to avenge Doll's imprisonment, he replies simply, grandly, heroically, 'I will deliver her' (39). And at that moment, the trumpets sound again (heralding the return procession of the now-crowned King Henry V) and Pistol comments, 'There roared the sea' (40), as if another natural force were active, as if the sea were released from a dam, as if the sea were angry . . .

Hal picks out Falstaff from the crowd and reprimands him. This could mean that Falstaff, in speaking to him first, is speaking out of turn. It could mean that the content of his speeches is indecorous. But it could also mean that Hal is using the opportunity (being now a master of timing and judgement) to display Falstaff to his people in the theatre of the streets and simultaneously display his own, new relationship with the man who is now his subject.

Falstaff addresses 'King Hal'. The formulation is awkward. It is not merely that he is trying to fuse informality with formality. He is also trying to adjust to the new reality, but he cannot do it. The Prince was Hal, the King is Henry. By saying 'Hal' Falstaff commits himself to the past. He is yesterday's man.

And then he says '*my* royal Hal!' (41). He presumes to own the King,

67

the King is his subject. Whereas the reverse is now true, he is Hal's subject. Pistol's 'imp' is not as discourteous as it sounds to our ears, but his phrase 'imp of fame' (43) calls attention neatly to the theme of reputation and public image. Hence, Falstaff's next speech 'God save thee, my sweet boy!' (44) seems the more ill-chosen. The king's public image is being tested and defined each time Falstaff opens his mouth. Is Hal still what his public image had been, Falstaff's favourite at the court of King Falstaff, and Falstaff his favourite? Or is he going to redefine his image? Falstaff calls him his sweet boy, his favourite, his darling, his child. Is Falstaff his father? No.

Hal speaks, for the first time as crowned monarch. The man he addresses is not his old seeming-father Falstaff, but the man he calls his new father, the Lord Chief Justice – '*My* Lord Chief Justice' (45). Falstaff he refuses to address at all, for Falstaff has no informal relationship with him now. Hal has taken up his true, royal identity, his political and historical identity, and Falstaff is left behind by events, by history and by the career and personal maturation of the man who is no longer Hal but King Henry.

The Lord Chief Justice asks Falstaff – 'Have you your wits? Know you what 'tis you speak?' (47–8). Falstaff had always prided himself on his wit, and believed himself wittier, smarter than the Lord Chief Justice. Now he is being a fool, proving himself unable to adapt to circumstances – which was, after all, his previous strength. But Falstaff can only speak what is in his heart, he has to go on making things worse, carried forward by his single-minded belief in his relationship with Hal. It is as if they really were father and son, and no one could argue him out of it. 'My King! My Jove! I speak to thee, my heart!' (49). *My* King, *my* God. But, at the same time, my *King*, my *God*. It is such troubling faith, a Protestant faith – no bishop, no priest, no intermediary, no Lord Chief Justice as go-between. 'I speak to thee, my heart.' Hal is his heart. But he is also speaking from his heart. It is pure love. Pederasty? Parenthood? But also son to father, subject to monarch, created to Creator. 'I know thee not, old man' (50).

In *Henry IV Part One* Hal had said 'I know you all' (I.ii.192). That was behind Falstaff's back. To his face, now, he pretends not even to know Falstaff's name. Why? Because he feels that Falstaff does not know *him*, does not know his nature and does not know his name, 'Henry'. Hal proposes a division between past and present, and a division between two selves, two identities, two 'Hals' – or, rather, a 'Hal' and a 'Henry'. Is 'I am' the same thing as 'I was' (59). No, for 'I' has turned away from Hal's 'former self' (61). And when 'I am' becomes again 'I have been' (63), *then* the new Falstaff ('thou shalt be') can again be the old Falstaff ('thou wast') (64). There are two Falstaffs now.

Hal calls upon further dualisms, too: waking and sleeping, reality and dreaming, reality and imagination.

> *I have long dreamt of such a kind of man . . .*
> *But being awaked I do despise my dream.*
>
> (52–4)

This is not the audience's experience, rejecting and despising the memory of Falstaff's scenes with Hal. But Hal has rejected his former self, as well as his dream. Falstaff is inevitably going to be swept away too.

Hal could be much harsher. He doesn't banish Falstaff from England, as his father had been banished by Richard II. In fact he isn't banished from any geographical spot. He is banished from court, 'our person' (68) – 'our' being the royal self, where 'I' was the private self. He is banished with 'the rest of my misleaders' (67), so it is not merely a rejection of Falstaff. And when Falstaff reforms himself he will be advanced (71–3).

Just as the new King's opening words were directed to the Lord Chief Justice, so too are his closing words. And, as he puts it, the Lord Chief Justice is to 'perform' the tenor of his 'word' (74). It is like a dramatist handing over his script to the actor.

Falstaff is humbled into dignity. He acknowledges his debt. He points out to Shallow that his promises were baseless and that he owes £1,000. Of the two, Shallow suddenly seems the less honourable man, demanding as he does the repayment of the debt.

Falstaff is broke. But the flame of his confidence in Hal is not out. 'I shall be sent for in private to him' (80). There are two Hals, the public and the private. That latter self still exists, he believes. It's just that 'he must seem thus to the world' (81). This may, of course, be true. It is certainly true that Hal is interested in his public image, his reputation, his fame. It may be, as he puts it, that the rejection is a 'colour' (89). But if Falstaff is wrong, Shallow points out, he has been banished on pain of death (66) and if he breaks his banishment in an attempt to see Hal in private, he will end up hung up in a collar (90).

Falstaff, the old Falstaff, the waking Falstaff rejecting the unpleasant dream, the nightmare of Hal's rejection, proposes an old remedy, food and camaraderie (91), and feels confident that Hal will summon him 'soon at night' (93) (Falstaff's time of day). But the Lord Chief Justice interrupts what *we* perceive as the dream, commanding the arrest of Falstaff and his friends and cutting short Falstaff's speech. Falstaff's last words in the play – indeed in the tetralogy – are, ironically enough, words of respect for the Lord Chief Justice, who has his triumph now: 'My lord, my lord –' (96).

Falstaff falls silent. The language of plot B is purged. ('I cannot now speak: I will hear you soon,' says the Lord Chief Justice at 97, and Pistol's linguistic extravagance is driven out. Prince John argues that in place of the 'conversations' (103) of Falstaff's world 'The king hath called his parliament' (106), a place devoted to the formal speech of plot A. John likes what he hears ('I heard a bird so sing,/ Whose music, to my thinking, pleased the King', at lines 110–11) and what he sees ('I like this fair proceeding of the King's', at line 100). The 'proceeding' was the procession, but it was also the rejection of Falstaff.

The ending is purely machiavellian. 'Civil swords' (109) will go to France, so that internal political problems are solved by attacking a foreign power. The idea was first put to Hal by his father at IV.v.213–14. At the time Hal made no comment. Now, we are told, it is an idea that pleases Hal. It is John who tells us this. Do we believe him? We have little choice. No more information is coming our way.

6. Summary of the Shape and Significance of Plot B

Once again, there is no single reading of plot B which all readers of it would agree on. But if we were obliged to plump for a central character and construct a narrative reading in terms of that character, it would have to be Falstaff.

He begins as a successful social climber, fresh from his triumph at Shrewsbury (where he claimed, entirely dishonestly, to have killed Hotspur and his claim was officially credited). He is celebrating by decking himself out in the fashionable accoutrements of a gentleman about town and he has aspirations to high office, having his eye on the key job of Lord Chief Justice in the next administration, when Hal becomes King Henry V. He crosses verbal swords with the man he considers to be his political rival, the present Lord Chief Justice. He then marches north in the King's service to help put down the northern rebellion, captures a 'famous rebel', Sir John Colevile of the Dale, and thereby further enhances his reputation as a soldier and loyal friend of the King's party. Having borrowed £1,000 from Justice Shallow, and on the news of King Henry's death, he rides to London in the belief that he will be made Lord Chief Justice, only to find himself publicly humiliated by the new King and committed to prison.

Plagued by gout, the pox, obesity and debt throughout the play, Falstaff follows a career that is, in formal terms, tragic (he loses his second skirmish with the Lord Chief Justice and all his successes are transformed into failure), in tonal terms pathetic, in moral terms a tale of thoroughly deserved ignominy. As criminal, traitor, rebel, misleader of youth, Satan, Ruffin, Riot, fool and jester he is brought to judgement and laughed out of court. As scapegoat he is victimized and driven out of society. As Vice he is vanquished by Virtue. As 'King' he is overthrown, usurped by the Lord Chief Justice. As 'Father' he is killed by his 'son'. As Carnival he is driven off the street. As Lord of Misrule his days are numbered. As Saturn, Mars and Cupid, he is shown up as mortal. As flesh he is spirited away. As embodiment of Life he is murdered.

7. What, No Hal Plot?

Combining the Two Plots

The distinction between plots A and B, which has been the foundation of this analysis, clearly breaks down in V.v. Here the two 'worlds', the world of the King and the world of Falstaff, come together. For the first time, Falstaff meets the King. The tension between the two plots appears to be formally resolved.

At the same time, however, the distinction between the two plots is reaffirmed. Falstaff may think that he is meeting the King, but the King, for his part, will not meet Falstaff: 'I know thee not, old man' (50). Indeed, the King commits himself to a greater severance of the two plots, acknowledging a kind of relationship in the past but relegating it to the world of fantasy and, in his own use of language, shifting away from even direct address to Falstaff: 'I have long dreamt of such a kind of man .../ But being awaked I do despise my dream' (52–4). We have a paradox, therefore. The paths of the two plots coincide in the street outside Westminster Abbey. The plots fuse. But they also refuse to fuse.

Of course, I have been calling plot A the 'King' plot because it represented the world of Henry IV. Falstaff never meets Henry IV in this play. He once attempted to address him in *Henry IV Part One* – at V.i.28 – but the gesture was rejected. The doctrine of the king's two bodies provides a model for the distinction which has always divided the two plots. Plot A, the King plot, concerned an office – that of the King; plot B, the Falstaff plot, concerned an individual, Falstaff. The union of the two plots is effected through the agency of a character who belongs to both but was never the major protagonist of either. In the 'theatrical' rite of passage which occupies the space between V.iv and V.v (i.e. the coronation), Hal's name changes to Henry V. This transformation, which can only be effected by a dramatist or by history, magically unites the two worlds of individual and office, and simultaneously provides plot A with a villain and plot B with a hero.

If we want to, we can say that the play as a whole has suddenly acquired a hero, a St George beating down the dragon Falstaff, an Oedipus speaking down the sphinx Falstaff, a Caesar triumphing in the street and entering the palace to rule. But if that is the reading we choose, where did he come from, this mysterious knight errant? We had a King plot, we had a Falstaff plot. Why did we have no Hal plot?

The answer is to be found in the rhetoric of this book. The absence of the Hal plot was trick, achieved by the sleight of hand whereby the play was presented as merely the sum of its plots. If the two halves of the puzzle are fitted back together again, if the multiple plot is re-assembled, the figure of Hal is discernible throughout.

The Induction requires an audience to recall what happened at the battle of Shrewsbury, which forms the climax of *Henry IV Part One*. There Hal killed the rebel Hotspur in single combat. Rumour explains that the truth is now to be distorted:

> *My office is*
> *To noise abroad that Harry Monmouth fell*
> *Under the wrath of noble Hotspur's sword . . .*
>
> (Induction, 28–30)

In this way the image of Hal's military virtue is reinforced in our minds. If this is Rumour's office, then the Induction establishes Hal as an absent presence from the start.

Within twenty lines of the opening of the next scene (I.i) Hal's name has been twice more invoked. We hear that 'The King is almost wounded to the death,/ . . . Prince Harry slain outright; . . ./ And Harry Monmouth's brawn, the hulk Sir John,/ Is prisoner'. This is then contradicted by the true report that a bloodied Hotspur actually rendered 'faint quittance, wearied and out-breathed,/ To Harry Monmouth, whose swift wrath beat down/ The never-daunted Percy to the earth'.

I.ii features Falstaff in his encounter with the Lord Chief Justice, but Falstaff's second speech informs us that his page boy was a gift from Hal, that 'the juvenal the Prince . . ., whose chin is not yet fledge' (19–20) is almost out of Falstaff's grace, because he is 'crowing as if he had writ man ever since his father was a bachelor' (25–6). At the entry of the Lord Chief Justice we are reminded of the story that he once 'committed the Prince for striking him' (53–4). The Lord Chief Justice accuses Falstaff of having 'misled the youthful Prince' (145–6) and of following 'the young Prince up and down, like his ill angel' (165–6). Falstaff's reply is pure cheek: 'The young Prince hath misled me . . . For the box of the ear that the Prince gave you, he gave it like a rude prince . . . I have checked him for it, and the young lion repents – [*aside*] marry, not in ashes and sackcloth, but in new silk and old sack' (147, 195–9).

73

LCJ: *Well, God send the Prince a better companion!*

FAL: *God send the companion a better prince! I cannot rid my hands of him.*

LCJ: *Well, the King hath severed you and Prince Harry. I hear you are going with Lord John of Lancaster against the Archbishop and the Earl of Northumberland.*

(200–207)

As the scene closes Falstaff is sending a letter to Hal asking for money. Thus Falstaff's relationship with Hal is suggested throughout this scene, and so too is Hal's relationship with the King. The northern rebels in I.iii provide the information that while the King is sending Prince John and Westmorland to face them, he has decided to pit 'Against the Welsh, himself and Harry Monmouth' (83).

In the tavern scene that follows (II.i) Mrs Quickly reminds Falstaff of the 'Wednesday in Wheeson week, when the Prince broke thy head for liking his father to a singing-man of Windsor' (86–8). Gower comes to the tavern door with the news that the King and Hal are near at hand, but Falstaff is urged by the Lord Chief Justice to go north quickly to join the army of Hal's brother.

II.ii is the first scene in which Hal appears but, as has been shown, we have been aware of his existence, his nature and his relationships in each of the preceding scenes. My argument in the earlier section of this book has been that II.ii is a part of a plot which focuses on Falstaff. And so it does. Its centrepiece is the reading of one of Falstaff's letters. But the letter is to Hal, and its arrival follows dialogue in which Poins accuses Hal of hypocrisy because he protests feeling for his father but has been in fact 'so lewd, and so much engraffed to Falstaff' (58–9). Clearly the scene concerns the relationships of Hal to both his father and Falstaff. It belongs to the Falstaff plot. But, in the context of the multiple plot, it contributes to the emerging plot of Hal.

II.iii reverts to the rebels, being the scene in which Northumberland is dissuaded by his wife and daughter-in-law from taking up arms against the King. However, once again, Hal is a reference point within the scene. The central speech is Lady Percy's description of Hotspur and his plight on Shrewsbury field. It ends bemoaning the fact that he had insufficient troops in his support – had he had more 'Today might I, hanging on Hotspur's neck,/ Have talked of Monmouth's grave' (44–5).

There follows the tavern scene in which Hal and Poins spy on Falstaff and Doll Tearsheet. The opening dialogue of the drawers is all about Falstaff and Hal. Falstaff is dominant as the only match for the violent Pistol and then as the wooer of Doll, but no sooner is Doll on his knee

74

than they fall to discussion of Hal. By this time Hal is himself literally upstaging Falstaff, having entered *'behind'* and, once Peto enters and the tone changes to matters solemn, Hal is entirely in command of events:

> *By heavens, Poins, I feel me much to blame,*
> *So idly to profane the precious time*
> *When tempest of commotion, like the south*
> *Borne with black vapour, doth begin to melt*
> *And drop upon our bare unarmèd heads.*
> *Give me my sword and cloak. Falstaff, good night.*
>
> (*Exeunt Prince and Poins*) (356–61)

The chill wind that will blow Falstaff away whips into the tavern as Hal opens the door and leaves. He leaves, we assume, to join his father, for Peto's message was that 'The King your father is at Westminster' (350). Thus, although Hal is never mentioned in the scene which follows (III.i), its subject-matter – the exhausted, guilt-laden, insomniac King in his distress that 'the body of our kingdom/ How foul it is, what rank diseases grow,/ And with what danger, near the heart of it' (38–40) – seems to point back to Hal in the tavern as much as north to the rebels. Similarly, despite the lack of any reference to Hal in the next scene (III.ii), in Shallow's orchard, its theme of the longing of the old for the life of their younger days not only echoes the King's longing for the lost state of innocence but reminds us of Hal's past when Falstaff sneers at Shallow's prating 'of the wildness of his youth' (294–5).

The next two scenes (IV.i and ii) work as one. Yet again, Hal is never mentioned but, as many commentators have argued, Prince John is his foil and there are significant references to 'boys and beggary', to 'surfeiting and wanton hours', to the King's foes being 'so enrooted with his friends', to the King being diverted from disciplining his subjects by the image of the 'infant' (IV.i.210), to the way in which a false favourite can misuse his prince's name (IV.ii.23–25). This run of scenes from III.i to IV.ii culminates in the moment when the King's son out-manoeuvres his enemies. The next scene, in which Falstaff yields his prisoner, Sir John Colevile of the Dale, to Prince John, closes with Falstaff's soliloquy on sack. This completes the run by presenting an account of Prince John that ends by contrasting the young, sober-blooded, demure boy with his hot-blooded elder brother. After the long silence about Hal, it comes as a relief to hear reference to him: 'Prince Harry is valiant' (IV.iii.115).

Although Hal is not physically present in IV.iv, it is devoted to the

75

King's impending death and his positive view of the Prince's qualities; Hal enters near the beginning of IV.v and the scene is then devoted to him and his relationship with his father.

V.i takes us back to Gloucestershire but Falstaff closes it with the intention of telling Hal about Shallow and thereby keeping him in continual laughter for a year. V.ii is the scene in which the new King Henry V establishes his new relationship with the Lord Chief Justice. In V.iii the news reaches Falstaff that his 'tender lambkin now is King' (116) and Falstaff sets off for London in the belief that 'the young King is sick for me' (133). The new administration is seen in action in V.iv as the beadles arrest Doll and Quickly, and V.v is the scene following the coronation and presents Hal's rejection of Falstaff.

Thus Hal is mentioned or present in fifteen scenes of the play. But his significance is much greater than this bald statement implies. The range of readings of plot A listed in my earlier section ('Summary of the Shape and Significance of Plot A', p. 38) hinges at least in part upon Hal. Any tragic reading would include the seemingly idle prince as an element in his father's suffering and punishment – the King fears the 'headstrong riot' which would characterize his son's reign (IV.iv.62); any comic (i.e. suggestive of Bolingbroke's ultimate political or personal success) reading would look to the reconciliations with the King (IV.v) and his Lord Chief Justice – 'You shall be as a father' (V.ii.118) – as the fulfilment of his reign. Similarly, in plot B, Falstaff's fortunes hinge ultimately upon his relationship with Hal. His reputation as a warrior derives from Hal's decision not to shop him over the supposed killing of Hotspur, and his ambitions to succeed at court (which give him the confidence to borrow money from Shallow and take on the Lord Chief Justice) are the consequences of his belief that Hal will always treat him as his favourite. Falstaff's tragic fall is the result of his ignorance of Hal's true nature.

Furthermore, there is a framework with reference to which we can, if we wish, interpret Hal's career. And that framework can be read as reinforcing the idea that this play has, as its overriding plot, a story in which Hal is a, if not the, protagonist. This framework is formed by the other history plays. We may decide to include any or all of the four plays discussed by C. W. R. D. Moseley in his Critical Study. And we may read them in a number of ways (Tillyard's way or Holderness's, for example). But if we know the play, it is going to be difficult to ignore the second scene of *Henry IV Part One* where, at its close, Hal slips into soliloquy, addressing his tavern companions who have just left the stage:

> *I know you all, and will awhile uphold*
> *The unyoked humour of your idleness.*
> *Yet herein will I imitate the sun,*
> *Who doth permit the base contagious clouds*
> *To smother up his beauty from the world,*
> *That when he please again to be himself,*
> *Being wanted, he may be more wondered at*
> *By breaking through the foul and ugly mists*
> *Of vapours that did seem to strangle him . . .*
> *So, when this loose behaviour I throw off . . .*
> *My reformation, glitt'ring o'er my fault,*
> *Shall show more goodly, and attract more eyes*
> *Than that which hath no foil to set it off.*
> *I'll so offend, to make offence a skill,*
> *Redeeming time when men think least I will.*

I.ii.192–215)

When the later play is seen in the context of its relationship to *Henry IV Part One*, Hal's significance seems multiple and supremely important. In terms of the King plot he is a constant source of anxiety and irritation, and he provides a symbolic expression of the King's political and personal problems. He is representative of the force that kills the individual mortal who aspired to power and achieved the supreme office. Yet he is also there to solve the King's personal and political problems, being reconciled with him at the end, allaying his fears, promising responsible rule and providing dynastic continuity. In terms of the Falstaff plot, Hal is the friend and protector but he is also the critic, the traitor and the judge. Neither plot could exist without him, he is ultimately the *other* factor in each. And when each play is seen whole and in the context of the other, Hal has a good claim to be regarded as the prime factor. From 'I know you all' to the rejection of Falstaff is as large an arch as that joining the King's opening speech in *Henry IV Part One* to his death in Act IV of *Henry IV Part Two*, or that joining Falstaff's first entry in *Henry IV Part One* to his exit in V.v in *Henry IV Part Two*.

Hal's position is contradictory here, as in the two plays taken together. 'I know you all' is soliloquy but, for all that, addressed to the absent Poins and Falstaff. If the play explores the structure of a morality play in which the Prodigal Son is tempted by Vice and eventually reforms, it is *Hal* who has written the morality play in which he seems

77

to be a player. He declares himself a Virtue in the second scene of *Henry IV Part One*, so his reformation in that play is a piece of play-acting. Having 'reformed' in *Henry IV Part One*, he is seemingly in need of re-reformation in *Henry IV Part Two*. Yet he would appear to be fully aware of Falstaff's nature, his own responsibilities and the fact that he is idling his time away. He tells Poins

By this hand, thou thinkest me as far in the devil's book as thou and Falstaff, for obduracy and persistency. Let the end try the man. But I tell thee, my heart bleeds inwardly that my father is so sick; and keeping such vile company as thou art hath in reason taken from me all ostentation of sorrow.

(II.ii.42–7)

What can explain the need for Hal's re-reformation? What can explain the fact that, if the play is about Hal and its theme is the solemn one of the education of a prince, so much of the play seems materially and tonally irrelevant?

We all enjoy a challenge and I would enjoy rising to this one. My explanation would be based on a kind of psychological-cum-anthropological reading of the play, and of all plays. It would go as follows.

A possible interpretation

The play is about the education of a princely psyche. Following Freud's practice in the interpretation of dreams, we would be justified in finding significance in the apparently insignificant. Education may be academic, but it may also be experiential, and the experience Hal undergoes may be symbolic as much as actual. Perhaps the satisfactions of drama as a medium for understanding the social and political life of an individual like Hal derive from its power to enact rituals in which rehearsed social experience and spontaneous individual experience work together. The narrative of Hal's career as it is told in *Henry IV Part Two* culminates in the public ritual of coronation but, except in Victorian productions of the play, the coronation is kept offstage. Instead, we are presented with an apparently unrelated and often bizarre set of incidents, some extending back beyond the boundaries of the play itself, even beyond the boundaries of any play Shakespeare wrote. Along with the killing of Hotspur from Part One there is the blow on the Lord Chief Justice's head from *The Famous Victories of Henry V*. The first clearly establishes Hal's credentials as a soldier and a loyal subject, the latter challenges authority and clearly leads to the complementary scene in Part

78

Two where Hal acknowledges that he is subject to the authority of the law and that his relationship to it is as that of a son to his father. The stealing of the crown and the King's notion that Hal hides a thousand daggers in his thoughts (IV.v.107) reinforce that pattern of recognition but also reveal the son's challenge to the father's authority.

Oddest of all the scenes in the Hal plot is II.iv. The 'heavy descension' (II.ii.168–9), the 'low transformation' (II.ii.170), the move 'From a prince to a prentice' (II.ii.169) are comparable to the famous scene in *Henry V* when Henry visits his troops in disguise the night before the battle of Agincourt. It is not difficult to interpret in political terms (the ideal prince must have the common touch and the ideal general must know the state of mind of his troops). But Hal explains his low transformation in II.iv as being like 'Jove's case' (II.ii.169) when he descended 'From a god to a bull' (II.ii.168). It may look like 'folly' (II.ii.171) but the folly must be weighed against 'the purpose' (II.ii.171) and the purpose would seem to have a sexual dimension. What Hal witnesses in II.iv is the doubly distasteful display of Falstaff's lechery and treachery. Little of this can be new to Hal, but the stage tableau of Hal voyeuristically studying 'Saturn and Venus in conjunction' is new to us.

The dramatic effectiveness of the scene largely derives from the sudden shift in tone with which it closes. A violent knocking on the door interrupts Hal as he is about to speak to Doll. The news of his father's illness renders Hal guilty.

> *By heaven, Poins, I feel me much to blame,*
> *So idly to profane the precious time*
> *When tempest of commotion, like the south*
> *Borne with black vapour, doth begin to melt*
> *And drop upon our bare unarmèd heads.*
> *Give me my sword and cloak. Falstaff, good night.*

(II.iv.356–61)

It is as if Hal were suddenly awake, shaken out of a lethargic dreamladen sleep – and he slips out of Falstaff's world as quickly as a dream.

This is the last we can see of Hal before he visits his father's deathbed, and the last Hal sees of Falstaff before he rejects him in the street. In Freudian terms, the scene in which Hal observes Falstaff making love to Doll could be regarded as a version of the 'primal scene', that occasion when a child witnesses, or imagines he witnesses, his parents'

79

copulation. That experience is universal, and a necessary stage in the development of the human psyche. It may be traumatic or it may be coped with. The Hal of *Henry IV Part Two* resembles Hamlet in his lethargy and world-weariness, his guilty feelings and his confusion over father-figures. Like Hamlet in the scene when he imagines his mother's copulation with a substitute-father (Claudius), Hal seems to have to endure this painful rite of passage before he can confront and 'kill' his fathers – Henry and Falstaff – and fulfil his princely destiny.

And yet. And yet. When *Henry IV Part Two* is seen on its own, Hal's absence from the main action of the play is peculiarly marked. He may be mentioned in the overwhelming majority of scenes, and certain scenes may be dominated by his presence, but in only five out of the play's twenty-one scenes is Hal actually *on* stage.

This last observation introduces an important issue. The physical presence of a character on stage has a significance for an audience which it can never have for someone reading the text in a book. Verbal allusions to that character by others must also make an impact, and in some scenes that impact may well be greater than mere physical presence. But even a silent, immobile presence registers in the theatre. In the printed text it can sometimes be neglected or forgotten.

It is important to remember that in our culture a play like *Henry IV Part Two* has a double life. It is both a printed text and a public performance. It is realized within two very different discourses, one 'literary' and the other 'theatrical'. This book, being merely a printed text itself and therefore best used at home or in the library, inevitably encourages concentration upon those aspects of the play which are literary rather than theatrical. But if we turn to consider the conditions under which the play has characteristically been performed over the years, some patterns emerge which throw light upon its distinctive nature.

There have been comparatively few notable professional productions of *Henry IV Part Two* as an independent play. An exception was the Stratford production by the famous actor-manager Frank Benson which began in 1894 and was repeated for a number of years thereafter. On the whole, though, directors have tended to present the play either in tandem with *Henry IV Part One*, or else as part of a longer sequence of history plays. In 1932 Stratford's newly built Shakespeare Memorial Theatre opened with productions of the two parts of *Henry IV* by W. Bridges-Adams, and fifty years later the Royal Shakespeare Company decided to mark the opening of its newly built London main house at the Barbican with productions of the same plays by Trevor Nunn. Meanwhile, in 1951, Stratford housed productions of the complete tetralogy of plays *Richard II* to *Henry V* (starring Richard Burton as Hal, Anthony Quayle as Falstaff and Harry Andrews as Henry IV). In 1964, the Royal Shakespeare Company staged the whole sequence of English history plays from *Richard II* to *Richard III*. John Barton ran both parts of *Henry IV* together with *Henry V* in a 1970 RSC 'Theatregoround' production and in 1991 Adrian Noble directed both parts of *Henry IV* at Stratford.

Outside Stratford, the same pattern is to be found. In 1986 Michael Bogdanov and Michael Pennington's English Shakespeare Company chose as its inaugural production *The Henrys*, i.e. both parts of *Henry IV* and *Henry V*. In 1987 they revived the same plays as part of the longer 'Wars of the Roses' cycle, which they proceeded to tour for two years.

Meanwhile, in the cinema and on television, *Henry IV Part Two* has never appeared as an isolated production unrelated to *Henry IV Part One* or, indeed, *Henry V*. In 1965 Orson Welles directed, and starred as Falstaff in, *Chimes at Midnight*, a film version of *Henry IV*, Parts One and Two, and *Henry V*. Five years earlier the play had formed an episode in Peter Dews's fifteen-part BBC television sequence of Shakespeare's English history plays *An Age of Kings*. In 1979 it appeared as part of a series which presented the whole of Shakespeare's dramatic output, the BBC/Time-Life 'Television Shakespeare'. As well as forming part of a thirty-seven-play sequence, it featured as the third production in a run of four broadcasts of the tetralogy *Richard II* to *Henry V*, with the same director and actors.

Thus, while *Henry V* is frequently and successfully performed on its own (the fine films by Laurence Olivier and Kenneth Branagh make the point), and while *Henry IV Part Two* is widely marketed on its own as a printed text, audio-recording or video-tape, it finds it difficult to stand alone in the theatre. To some extent recent directors have probably been influenced by literary critics who, particularly since E. M. W. Tillyard's *Shakespeare's History Plays* of 1944, have argued that the history plays are to be read as a whole and express a statement about English nationhood or the nature of politics. For example, in his Penguin Critical Study, *Shakespeare's History Plays, 'Richard II' to 'Henry V': The Making of a King*, Charles Moseley claims that the 'Henriad' is about 'the maturing of a prince' and 'the education of the ideal prince' (p. 131). But this has not prevented directors extracting other plays from the sequence, particularly *Richard II* and *Henry V*, and presenting them on their own.

If *Henry IV Part Two* is conceived of as being a stage in 'the maturing of a prince', its function is to look forward to the play in which that prince's maturity is displayed, *Henry V*. The unifying element in its structure thereby becomes a particular character, Hal, who also becomes the focus for a unity which is thematic. In the English Shakespeare Company's 1986 and 1987 productions Michael Pennington played Hal and, being noticeably too old for the character in *Henry IV*, the awkwardness of his performance provided a dynamic sense of direction for the sequence as a whole, since he proved to be entirely comfortable in the role of the 'mature' Henry V when it came along.

But if we read *Henry IV Part Two* in isolation, the notion that Hal has a structural centrality as a character becomes more problematic. It also becomes hard to argue that the play deals with the specific theme of princely education except in patches. Indeed, one could make the case that Shakespeare has organized his play around quite other themes, and many critics have done so. For example, one could easily claim for it a unity deriving from a concern with such things as disease, corruption or miscalculation. In his 1959 essay, 'Times Subjects: *2 Henry IV*', L. C. Knights wrote of this 'tragi-comedy of human frailty' that it was about 'age, disappointment and decay' (in G. K. Hunter, *Shakespeare: 'Henry IV Parts 1 and 2'*, 1970, p. 174).

When Part Two is produced or read in conjunction with *Richard II* and *Henry IV Part One* it becomes possible to find unity in the person of Henry Bolingbroke, so that Part Two provides the punishment for the guilt he feels for the usurpation of Richard's throne. Hal can then be read as a complementary source of unity, for he provides the opportunity for the expiation of his father's guilt. Even without recourse to *Richard II*, a director can point up such a unifying theme. Early-nineteenth-century performances introduced enormous pageantry into the play when Hal becomes king in V.v, and Macready's 1821 production at Covent Garden included four extra scenes 'displaying the grand Coronation'.

But if Part Two is linked solely with Part One, Hal's significance shifts and the rejection of Falstaff provides the culmination of the process whereby he clarifies his relationship not only with his father and the crown but with his private self, his friends, his past and his people. At the same time, the focus clearly shifts some way towards Falstaff as a source – and possibly the major source – of unity. The rejection provides a denouement to his personal history and completes the story of his decline from comic invulnerability. But it also exposes the human price paid by Hal and his nation for the resolution of political conflict. A. C. Bradley's famous essay of 1902 (perhaps the most famous thing ever written about the play), 'The Rejection of Falstaff', argues that our feelings during the rejection scene must include pain and resentment and traces the source of those feelings back to earlier scenes. He assumes that we have 'keenly enjoyed' the earlier Falstaff scenes and he makes clear that he means the Falstaff scenes 'of the two plays' (in Hunter, op. cit., p.59).

When Part Two is produced or read on its own, the absence of Part One's Falstaff scenes is bound to alter the balance of feeling and ideas which Bradley describes. But the process of feeling and ideas which makes up the play is also bound to be affected by the absence of all the other scenes which make up Part One, and indeed all the scenes which make up any of the plays which directors or critics have ever called upon in order to find meaning in Part Two.

The more one attempts to isolate *Henry IV Part Two* and treat it as a distinct entity unrelated to other plays in the sequence, the more difficult it becomes as a subject for interpretation. That difficulty is in part the difficulty presented by the assertion of unpalatable truths – the bleak truths represented by the callous treatment of the recruits by Falstaff, the rebels by Prince John, the King by guilt, Doll by the officers, Falstaff by Hal and everybody by time and death. But the difficulty is also the difficulty presented by the play's refusal to resolve the contradictions built into its structure.

The rejection scene is an exemplar of this difficulty, for here the sense of unresolved contradiction is at its most exposed. V.v is the dramatic and theatrical climax of the play, the place where all the polarized components – old and young, Gloucestershire and Cheapside, public and private, king and subject, history and fiction, plot A and plot B – finally meet. And the result is mere contradiction, a rejection of resolution. Hal rejects the idea that he can communicate with Falstaff ('I know thee not'), Falstaff finds he has nothing to say (he is reduced to 'My lord, my lord –') and the Lord Chief Justice admits, 'I cannot now speak.'

Significantly enough, the last word of the scene goes to Prince John, the man whose word we have learned from the bitter experience of Gaultree not to trust. More significant for this book, however, is the ambiguous comment which John makes on the meeting of Hal and Falstaff which we have just witnessed. He calls it a 'fair proceeding'. We are left to ponder whether 'fair' indicates John's moral or aesthetic satisfaction with the meeting of the two plots. Either meaning raises the difficult question: is it possible entirely to agree or disagree?

Appendix: An Outline of the Multiple Plot

Induction A symbolic figure personifying 'Rumour' informs the audience that he is spreading false reports of the battle of Shrewsbury (1403), at which King Henry IV confronted rebel armies led by Henry ('Hotspur') Percy and Archibald, Earl of Douglas.

I.i At Warkworth Castle just such a rumour reaches Hotspur's father, the Earl of Northumberland, who has missed the battle by feigning sickness. Lord Bardolph has brought him the news, conveyed to him by a respectable gentleman hot-foot from the battle, that Hotspur has killed Prince Hal and captured Hal's favourite, Sir John Falstaff, that the King's supporters have fled and that the King himself is mortally wounded. But Northumberland's spirits are immediately dashed by a second report, this time from a servant who has spoken with another gentleman leaving the battle: the rebels are in fact defeated and Hotspur is dead, killed by Prince Hal. This report is now confirmed by Morton, an eyewitness at the battle. Northumberland is fired by his grief to set to work and launch another wave of rebellion, this time in support of the Archbishop of York, who is leading an army against the King, committed to avenge the death of Richard II (whom Henry IV had deposed).

I.ii The Lord Chief Justice wants Sir John Falstaff to explain why he never responded to a summons to appear and explain his part in the Gadshill robbery (dramatized in *Henry IV Part One*). But Falstaff's reputation as a military hero (a reputation solely based on Falstaff's spurious claim to have killed the rebel Harry Hotspur at the battle of Shrewsbury – another incident drawn from *Part One*) has saved his skin, and anyway he is now required to join Prince John's army against a rebellion in the north led by the Earl of Northumberland and the Archbishop of York.

I.iii Some of the rebels (the Archbishop, Thomas Mowbray the Earl Marshal, Lord Hastings and Lord Bardolph) meet. They already have 25,000 men, but there is some disagreement between them as to whether, without the further support of Northumberland and his men, they are strong enough to take on the loyalist forces. The conclusion is that, since the King's troops are already having to cope with Glendower's forces in Wales and a French army as well, they have the advantage over them. The Archbishop urges them to advance, sensing that the common people have already grown tired of Henry Bolingbroke's reign and will support a movement inspired by the memory of Richard II, whom Bolingbroke dethroned.

II.i Mistress Quickly, hostess of the Boar's Head tavern in Cheapside, London, has initiated a lawsuit against Falstaff for the hundred marks he owes her. When Falstaff enters with Bardolph he is arrested by two officers and then ordered by the Lord Chief Justice to repay Quickly what he owes her. In fact Falstaff succeeds in persuading her to lend him still more money. The Lord Chief Justice urges him to get on with recruiting soldiers and march north.

II.ii Hal confesses to his friend Poins that, for all his apparent neglect of princely duties, he lacks enthusiasm for his current lifestyle and is inwardly upset at his father's illness. When Bardolph enters with a letter from Falstaff to Hal, a letter whose cheek irritates not only Hal but Poins as well, they decide to play a trick on Falstaff by disguising themselves as drawers at the Boar's Head and spying on Falstaff's liaison with a prostitute, the notorious Doll Tearsheet.

II.iii Northumberland's wife and daughter-in-law are pleading with him not to go to war with the King. The latter contemptuously reminds him how he failed to support Harry Hotspur (his son and her husband) at his hour of need by failing to make an appearance at the battle of Shrewsbury. Neither woman wants him to risk his life in the way that Hotspur did, making armed rebellion with insufficient troops to support him. Northumberland feels his honour is at stake but wavers, and finally decides to wait in Scotland and see how the rebellion fares.

II.iv The Boar's Head. Quarrels and scuffles break out involving two customers the worse for drink – Doll Tearsheet and a well-known hooligan (or 'swaggerer'), Pistol. Falstaff drives the latter out and is rewarded for his gallantry and courage by some dalliance with the former. But Hal and Poins, who play a practical joke on Falstaff by disguising themselves as bartenders ('drawers') and observing the erotic scene, find that Falstaff is slandering them to Doll. They drop their disguises and confront Falstaff with his dishonourable conduct. He attempts to argue himself out of this scrape but is saved further embarrassment by the arrival of news that he is summoned to court to prepare to fight the rebels mustering in the north. Hal feels pangs of guilt at his irresponsible behaviour at a time of national crisis.

III.i For the first time we see King Henry. It is 1 a.m., but he is unable to sleep, being oppressed not only by his recent illness but now also by his anxiety over the threatened rebellion in the north.

III.ii Falstaff is in the Gloucestershire countryside. It is early morning and he has arranged to recruit soldiers from the household of Master Robert Shallow, a country JP and fellow student at Clement's Inn fifty-five years earlier. Shallow is near-senile and gullible and, once Falstaff has signed up a motley collection of country bumpkins, and then been bribed by some of them to let them go after all, he accepts Shallow's invitation to drop in again on his way back from the wars, knowing there will be money to make out of his old college acquaintance.

IV.i The Forest of Gaultree, eight miles north of York. Archbishop Scroop is telling Mowbray and Hastings that Northumberland has written that he has gone to Scotland and cannot join the rebellion at this time. News arrives that Prince John's army of 30,000 men are now less than a mile west of the forest. Westmorland comes to speak with them, arguing that their grievances are insufficient to justify armed rebellion and that Prince John is prepared to listen to them on behalf of his father and satisfy any just demands they make. Scroop provides him with a written account of their demands and Westmorland withdraws temporarily to consult with John. The rebels are in disagreement about whether or not to trust the King, but accept the offer of a parley when Westmorland returns.

IV.ii The parley. We meet John for the first time. After an aggressive initial interchange between the two sides John declares that the rebels' grievances 'shall be with speed redressed,/ Upon my soul, they shall'. The rebels fall for this offer and disband their army. Whereupon John arrests them, defending his promise that their grievances would be redressed by divorcing the grievances from the grievers (the substance from the form) and redressing them in different ways. He will put right the former but have the latter executed as traitors.

IV.iii Meanwhile, in another part of the forest, Falstaff succeeds in taking prisoner one of the rebel knights, Sir John Colevile of the Dale. Falstaff shows a lack of cowardice here that we might not have expected, but it is his (false) reputation as the hero of Shrewsbury (when he claimed, and was allowed by Hal to get away with it, that he had killed Hotspur) that persuades Colevile to surrender to him. Falstaff boasts of his achievement (quoting Julius Caesar's *veni, vidi, vici*). Prince John is perceptibly unimpressed, and presses on with his business, sending Colevile on to York to be executed with the other rebel leaders and setting off for London himself. Left alone, Falstaff muses on the virtues of sack for a while, before departing for Gloucestershire again.

IV.iv The Jerusalem Chamber in Westminster Abbey, London. Two of the King's sons, Thomas, Duke of Clarence, and Humphrey, Duke of Gloucester, are with their father, who is extremely ill. He has been making arrangements so that, once the rebellion is over, he can lead a crusade. Meanwhile, he is worried to hear from Thomas that Hal is not hunting at Windsor, as Humphrey believes, but with Poins in London and therefore, presumably, leading a dissolute life still. Warwick tries to reassure him that this lifestyle is part of Hal's education and that, in time, he will outgrow his enjoyment of it and put his knowledge of it to advantage. Westmorland brings news of the putting down of the northern rebellion (including the death of Northumberland at the battle of Bramham Moor). The news is wonderful for the King but he suddenly feels very ill and swoons in an apoplectic fit.

IV.v They carry the King into an adjoining room, where he lies on a bed with the crown on his pillow beside his head. Hal arrives and is left alone with his sleeping father. But his father appears not to be breathing and Hal suddenly believes him to be dead. He takes the crown from the pillow, puts it on his head and wanders out of the room. The King wakes up, calling for his courtiers, and then discovers that his crown has disappeared. He assumes that Hal has taken it, greedy for power. When Hal comes back and they are left alone with each other, the King launches an attack on Hal's riotous lifestyle and the apparent haste with which he would seize power. Hal protests his innocence of such accusations, and his father is reconciled to him. The King confesses his guilt over the usurpation of Richard II's throne and warns Hal against trust in political supporters, advising him to wage war abroad in order to secure unity at home. Prince John arrives from the north, but only in time to hear his father prophesy his own imminent death. The King sees the wit in dying in the Jerusalem Chamber, since it had always been said that he 'should not die but in Jerusalem', and so he is carried back into the room next door.

V.i Back in Gloucestershire, Falstaff is being entertained by Shallow, who hopes that by wining and dining Falstaff he will thereby gain a foothold at court.

V.ii In London the Earl of Warwick informs the Lord Chief Justice that the King is dead. Hal's three brothers sympathize with the Lord Chief Justice, who, everyone agrees, is bound to lose his job. This is because he once had the temerity to arrest Hal for thieving and then imprison him when Hal punched him on the head. Hal enters. The new King sees fear, as well as grief, in their faces. But he assures them they are safe. Even the Lord Chief Justice is told his job is secure because he had the courage and impartiality to treat Hal like any other subject. He announces that the days of his wildness are over. He will summon Parliament and choose wise counsellors to advise him.

V.iii Falstaff has been wined and dined, and is strolling in Shallow's orchard before turning in for the night. In his cups Justice Silence has finally found his voice, singing old drinking songs. But their carousing is interrupted by Pistol's arrival from London. He brings the news of the old King's death and the accession of Hal. Falstaff instantly believes that his career is made, for surely Hal will appoint him Lord Chief Justice in place of their old enemy. They prepare to leave for London.

V.iv In Cheapside a moral purge has been instigated. The beadles are arresting Doll and Mrs Quickly following the death of a man beaten up by them and Pistol.

V.v In the street outside Westminster Abbey, the new King processes to his coronation. Falstaff, Shallow, Pistol and Bardolph are in the crowd, full of anticipation that, once crowned, Hal will promote Falstaff. But when the coronation procession comes out of the Abbey and Falstaff calls out to 'King Hal' from the crowd, 'King Henry V' tells him that, though his life is spared, Falstaff is no longer to be allowed within ten miles of him until he undergoes a moral reformation. The royal procession moves on. Falstaff had borrowed a thousand pounds from Shallow in anticipation of his promotion. Now Shallow demands it back. Falstaff is momentarily crushed by Hal's snub, but he is soon convincing himself – if no one else – that it was a public-relations tactic to seem to be rejecting him and that, come evening, the new King will be inviting him to a private audience. The Lord Chief Justice interrupts this reverie, however, arresting Falstaff and all his companions and sending them to the Fleet prison. Prince John expresses satisfaction at Hal's style of government, and prophesies that within the year an English army will have invaded France.

Epilogue This promises to continue the story in another play, mentioning as attractions Falstaff and Princess Katherine of France.

Further Reading

The references in this book are all to P. H. Davison's New Penguin Shakespeare edition (Harmondsworth, Penguin Books, 1977). You will find that A. R. Humphreys's Arden Shakespeare edition (London, Methuen, 1966) and Giorgio Melchiori's New Cambridge Shakespeare edition (Cambridge, CUP, 1989) are also scholarly and helpful.

For criticism of the play and discussion of relevant material you might turn first to the following:

W. H. Auden, 'The Prince's Dog', *The Dyer's Hand*, London, 1963 (in Hunter, 1970)

C. L. Barber, *Shakespeare's Festive Comedy: A Study of Dramatic Form and its Relation to Social Custom*, New Jersey, Princeton University Press, 1959

A. C. Bradley, 'The Rejection of Falstaff', *Oxford Lectures on Poetry*, London, Macmillan, 1909 (in Hunter, 1970)

M. D. Bristol, *Carnival and Theater: Plebeian Culture and the Structure of Authority in Renaissance England*, London, Methuen, 1985

J. L. Calderwood, *Metadrama in Shakespeare's Henriad*, Berkeley, University of California Press, 1979

Terry Eagleton, *William Shakespeare*, Oxford, Blackwell, 1986

William Empson, 'Double Plots', *Some Versions of Pastoral*, London, Chatto and Windus, 1935

Graham Holderness, *Richard II*, Harmondsworth, Penguin Books (Penguin Critical Studies), 1989

Graham Holderness, *Shakespeare's History*, Dublin, Gill & Macmillan, 1985

Graham Holderness, John Turner and Nick Potter, *Shakespeare: The Play of History*, London, Macmillan, 1988

G. K. Hunter, '*Henry IV* and the Elizabethan Two-Part Play', *Review of English Studies*, new series V, 1954

G. K. Hunter, *Shakespeare: 'Henry IV Parts 1 and 2'*, London, Macmillan (Casebook series), 1970

Harold Jenkins, *The Structural Problem in Shakespeare's 'Henry IV'*, London, Methuen, 1956

Critical Studies: Henry IV Part Two

D. S. Kastan, *Shakespeare and the Shapes of Time*, London, Macmillan, 1982

H. A. Kelly, *Divine Providence in the England of Shakespeare's Histories*, Cambridge, Mass., Harvard University Press, 1970

R. A. Law, 'Structural Unity in the Two Parts of *Henry IV*', *Studies in Philology* XXIV, 1927

Richard Levin, *The Multiple Plot in English Renaissance Drama*, Chicago, Chicago University Press, 1971

C. Leech, 'The Unity of *2 Henry IV*', *Shakespeare Survey* VI, 1953

A. A. Mendilow, 'Falstaff's Death of a Sweat', *Shakespeare Quarterly* IX, no. 4, Autumn 1958

Maurice Morgann, *An Essay on the Dramatic Character of Sir John Falstaff* (1777), critical edition by D. A. Fineman, Oxford, OUP, 1972

C. W. R. D. Moseley, *Shakespeare's History Plays, 'Richard II' to 'Henry V': The Making of a King*, Harmondsworth, Penguin Books (Penguin Critical Studies), 1988

M. E. Prior, *The Drama of Power: Studies in Shakespeare's History Plays*, Evanston, Illinois, Northwestern University Press, 1973

Irving Ribner, *The English History Play in the Age of Shakespeare*, Princeton University Press, 1957

P. Saccio, *Shakespeare's English Kings: History, Chronicle and Drama*, Oxford, OUP, 1977

M. A. Shaaber, 'The Unity of *Henry IV*', in *John Quincy Adams Memorial Studies*, ed. McManaway, Washington, 1948

K. Smidt, *Unconformities in Shakespeare's History Plays*, London, Macmillan, 1982

B. Spivack, 'Falstaff and the Psychomachia', *Shakespeare Quarterly* VIII, 1957

J. I. M. Stewart, *Character and Motive in Shakespeare*, London, Longman, Green, 1949 (extract in Hunter, 1970)

E. M. W. Tillyard, *Shakespeare's History Plays*, London, Chatto & Windus, 1944

V. Traub, 'Prince Hal's Falstaff: Positioning Psychoanalysis and the Female Reproductive Body', *Shakespeare's Quarterly* 40, iv, 1989

D. A. Traversi, *Shakespeare: From 'Richard II' to 'Henry V'*, London, Hollis & Carter, 1957

Brian Vickers, *The Artistry of Shakespeare's Prose*, London, Methuen, 1970

J. S. Wilders, *The Lost Garden: A View of Shakespeare's English and Roman History Plays*, London, Macmillan, 1978

J. Dover Wilson, *The Fortunes of Falstaff*, Cambridge, CUP, 1943